The Media Effect

**Recent Titles in
Democracy and the News**

Editorial and Opinion: The Dwindling Marketplace of Ideas in Today's News
Steven M. Hallock

No Questions Asked: News Coverage since 9/11
Lisa Finnegan

The Media Effect

How the News Influences Politics and Government

Jim Willis

Democracy and the News

Jeffrey Scheuer, Series Editor

Westport, Connecticut
London

Library of Congress Cataloging-in-Publication Data

Willis, William James, 1946-
   The media effect : how the news influences politics and government / Jim Willis.
     p. cm. — (Democracy and the news, 1932–6947)
   Includes bibliographical references and index.
   ISBN–13: 978–0–275–99496–9 (alk. paper)
   ISBN–10: 0–275–99496–1 (alk. paper)
1. Government and the press—United States. 2. Press and politics—United States. I. Title.
PN4738.W55 2007
302.230973—dc22   2007010318

British Library Cataloguing in Publication Data is available.

Library of Congress Catalog Card Number: 2007010318
ISBN–13: 978–0–275–99496–9
ISBN–10: 0–275–99496–1
ISSN: 1932–6947

First published in 2007

Praeger Publishers, 88 Post Road West, Westport, CT 06881
An imprint of Greenwood Publishing Group, Inc.
www.praeger.com

Printed in the United States of America

The paper used in this book complies with the
Permanent Paper Standard issued by the National
Information Standards Organization (Z39.48–1984).

10 9 8 7 6 5 4 3 2 1

For Joe Hight
of *The Oklahoman*
A fine friend, a fine editor

Contents

Series Foreword *by Jeffrey Scheuer*	ix
Preface	xi
(1) Media Impact on Government: Views Vary	1
(2) The Media and Political Action	15
(3) The Media and National Development	29
(4) How Events and Issues Become News	43
(5) What the Research Reveals	55
(6) Decoding the News: A Primer in Media Literacy	73
(7) Politicians and Journalists: A Symbiotic Relationship	93
(8) Presidents and the Press	105
(9) Conducting War in a Media Age	117
(10) The Media as the Fourth Estate	137
Notes	147
Selected Bibliography	155
Index	157

Series Foreword

It doesn't require much study of the mass media to realize just how complex the subject is, or why it fascinates. The media, collectively speaking, are both literal and figurative prisms. As imperfect lenses through which we perceive nearly all of politics and social life, they are not stable, isolated elements within society; but neither do they stand wholly outside of it. Instead, they are part of a vast and evolving ecosystem of tools and techniques, actions and events, ideas and perceptions. As necessary instruments for accessing life on a larger scale than personal experience, the media forever straddle the boundary between what we perceive and how we perceive it.

One result of this is a binocular effect, a kind of necessary double-vision, as we seek at once to understand how things really are and, at the same time, how the media's reproductions – what Jim Willis, following Walter Lippmann, calls the "shadow world" – shape and are shaped by the "outer world" they aim to reproduce. We try to see the world clearly as if from the outside, but we also swim in it; and as Marshall McLuhan said, whoever discovered water, it wasn't a fish.

This disparity between the mediated and unmediated realms, noted by Lippmann in *Public Opinion* (1922), remains problematic. As Willis concisely explains in his Preface: "The pictures we have in our heads about the way our world operates fuel our behavioral reactions which take place not in a world of images (a shadow world) but in the very real world."

The study of media is a confrontation with this dilemma (or set of dilemmas) at various levels. There are many possible angles of approach, and many subjects of potential interest or concern: one might consider, for example, the functions and effects of particular media, or their comparative or historical use, or their role in shaping specific issues or phenomena. There are advantages to specificity and also to breadth.

In *The Media Effect*, Willis addresses various aspects of the web of cause-and-effect between the political realm and the media. Among other things, he usefully spotlights the issues of war, the presidency, agenda-setting, ideological skewing and bias, public relations, the news consumer and media literacy, how "the news" is formed, and how journalists and politicians interact. It is a rich gamut.

Willis's basic premise is foundational to all media studies: that the media have both visible and invisible effects on what they mediate, skewing perceptions and actions. Like much of the best media scholarship, this book is an attempt to render visible the unseen. And in treating a range of important political dimensions, it addresses questions directly pertinent to this series on Democracy and the News.

As both an experienced journalist and an established scholar (a too-rare combination), Jim Willis is well positioned for the complex enterprise of rendering the media's shadows visible. His panoramic approach here reminds us how important clear double-vision is to understanding the media, and how important such understanding is for using the levers of democracy.

Jeffrey Scheuer
Series Editor

Preface

In 1990 I wrote a book titled, *The Shadow World: Life Between the News Media and Reality*. In that book I picked up on the thinking of journalists such as Walter Lippmann, who wrote early in the twentieth century about "the world outside and the pictures in our heads." Lippmann posited that most of what we think we know of the outside world—those snippets and images and thoughts which are the pictures in our heads—are put there by the news media. He reminded us—as have semanticists and semiologists through the ages—that the word (or even the picture) is not the thing; the map is not the territory. The pictures in our heads and what may be going on in the real world could be similar or vastly different.

Writing this in 1922, Lippmann was talking exclusively about the print media. What was true then is geometrically more true today as the print media have been joined—if not overtaken—by radio, television, and now the World Wide Web. Today we have more sources for those pictures in our heads than ever before, yet does that mean we have a truer understanding of what is actually happening in our world? Not necessarily. Is this important? Vitally. Why? Because the pictures we have in our heads about the way our world operates fuels our behavioral reactions, which take place not in a world of images (a shadow world) but in the very real world. We elect the right or the wrong people to government in the real world, we make decisions on how to spend our tax money in the real world, and we go to war in the real world.

This is a book about the pictures in our heads of government and politicians, and how these media-originated pictures influence decisions and actions of government leaders and politicians. Nowhere is a journalist's responsibility heavier than in the accurate representation of those people whom we elect into office to lead us over the next two, four, or six years. But it is also a study in how politicians and government leaders relate to the journalists who cover them on a daily basis. Further, a portion of the book deals with that most deadly decision which government leaders make and politicians debate: going to war and, once there, how to conduct the war. Readers should note a definite change in the dynamics between the media and the military in the guidelines and rules set up for the press to follow in covering these wars. Part of the changes that have taken place regarding these rules has come from the realization by government officials that it is very hard to conduct a sustained war under the scrutiny of the news media. Journalists, as always, want to do an objective job of reporting what is going on, but politicians and government leaders would rather have them report only the positives that happen, especially during times of war.

One chapter in this book will look at how a few of the 43 presidents have dealt with the media and the reasons for their treatment of—and by—the press. Over the course of American history, different presidents have treated the media in different ways and have been on the receiving end of some scathing stories and commentaries.

In a democracy, sometimes described skeptically as the worst kind of government on earth...except for all the rest, both politicians and journalists are necessary. If we're going to have elections, we have to have candidates to choose from, and the winning candidates become our government leaders. To get to know these candidates and the issues they are discussing, we need the news media. In this, President Thomas Jefferson was right when he said that given the choice between a free government and a free press, he would not hesitate to choose the latter, because a free press is a guarantor of a free government. Does that mean that both institutions of government and the media always work well? Always live up to their potential? Certainly not. We are talking about reality, after all. But it does mean the ideals do exist and that as long as America is free, the best of the politicians and the best of the journalists will be striving to reach those lofty, idealistic goals. In that journey, the media and the politicians find something interesting: they both need each other.

One chapter of this book analyzes the very real and symbiotic relationship that occurs between journalists and politicians. In America, the news media have elevated politics to the most important of the national news beats. But even at the local level, politics at City Hall is always an important story. So journalists need the politicians and officeholders to "feed the beast" of the daily news hole, which has become a minute-by-minute news hole on live television and the Web. And, on their side, politicians need journalists to help them get the headlines and airtime they crave. The trick is for politicians to focus on the issues and the public good, and for journalists to do an objective job in covering the politicians and the issues. The temptation, which too often becomes reality, is for the "dance" between journalists and politicians to become more important: for each side to pander too much to the other in search of getting what each side needs from the other.

Another chapter in this book will survey some of the more recent and interesting research done into the role the news media play in setting agendas for public discussion and the role they play in helping to shape public opinion, often by elevating issues to the plane of public discussion.

As with any book, I am grateful to the many writers and researchers who have analyzed different aspects of how the news media influences politics and the government. I draw from many of their works in this project. I am also grateful to my university for allowing me time over the past year to pull this material together. On a personal level, I am most grateful to my loving wife Anne who has shown extreme patience at home in allowing me to focus on this project as much as I have.

. . .Jim Willis

CHAPTER 1

Media Impact on Government: Views Vary

The year: 2007

The issue: Medical treatment by military hospitals of returning U.S. soldiers, wounded in the wars in Iraq and Afghanistan.

The media report: The *Washington Post* concludes a four-month investigation into the sub-standard medical treatment of wounded soldiers returning from combat. *Post* reporters Dana Priest and Anne Hull break the first of the two-part series of February 18, under the headline, "Soldiers Face Neglect, Frustration at Army's Top Medical Facility."[1] Within several days, other national media like *Newsweek* and ABC are on the story of questionable medical treatment of returning vets. *Newsweek* carries an eight-page cover story on the issue, and on February 26, ABC airs a special one-hour report called "To Iraq and Back," chronicling newsman Bob Woodruff's severe cranial wound received when a bomb exploded near his vehicle in Baghdad. Woodruff devotes part of his report to questioning the after-care treatment of returning wounded soldiers, although he focuses on the nation's Veterans Affairs hospitals.

The reaction: In the immediate wake of these stories, the two-star general in charge of Walter Reed Army Medical Center is relieved of his command by the secretary of the Army over questions about his abilities to improve out-patient care for the most serious of cases at Walter Reed.[2] Historically, this facility has been the preeminent military hospital in America. The day after the general was fired, the Secretary of the Army who relieved him of his command is also fired over the same issue.

The year: 2005.

The issue: Security of U.S. seaports.

The media report: The White House announces President Bush will sign a deal turning over the responsibility for securing major U.S. seaports to a company recently purchased by the United Arab Emirates.

The reaction: Public opinion in America rises quickly and strongly against a Middle Eastern company providing security for its vulnerable seaports in the post-9/11 climate. Members of Congress and Bush find themselves on opposite sides of the question of whether U.S. port security would be compromised by an Arab company's takeover of operations at six major American ports. Some congress members, even Republicans, warn that the safeguards are not enough to prevent infiltration of the seaports by terrorists. The majority of Congress rises in protest to the idea, with key congressional Republicans protesting the plan as well. President Bush mounts a weak effort to defend his plan, saying the company's integrity and history speak for itself. Soon, however, he decides to give into Congressional pressure to abandon the idea.

The year: 1997.

The debate: A UN-sponsored treaty that would ban the use of land mines around the globe. A Vermont-based advocacy group, the Campaign to Ban Land Mines, takes a decisive role in backing the proposed treaty. The United States government, however, opposes it. The advocacy organization presses its campaign to outlaw the use of mines by going to the World Wide Web to announce and explain its stance and to bring together more than a hundred different advocacy groups around the world to support the proposed treaty.

The result: The treaty is adopted in December of 1997. The organizer of the advocacy campaign supporting the treaty, Jody Williams, received the Nobel Prize in 1998 for her tireless efforts.

In his book, *Digital Diplomacy*, Wilson P. Dizard notes the following about the importance of the Web in getting this treaty adopted and in pushing the government for other changes as well:

> The land mine campaign involved a temporary Web page alliance by like-minded groups to deal with a single event. More recently, such networking has taken on a more permanent institutional cast. The trend of toward forming ongoing public policy networks covering a wide range of cross-border issues, from the eradication of malaria to the depletion of global fishing grounds...They (the networks) are run by groups that thrive in a borderless environment, capitalizing on the World Wide Web's interactive capabilities.[3]

The year: 1994.

The battleground: The central market district in Sarajevo on February 5.

The media report: A 120-mm mortar shell is fired into the crowded market-place on one of the busiest days of the year. Sixty-eight people die and over

200 are injured. The round explodes waist-high and there is carnage everywhere. It is all recorded in real time by television cameras.

The reaction: President Bill Clinton immediately calls for an end to the U.S. policy of non-involvement in the Balkans and leads NATO in demanding that the Bosnian Serbs remove all heavy weaponry from around the Bosnian capital. It also leads to the creation of a five-member international coalition to find a diplomatic solution to the Bosnian violence.

The year: 1990.

The place: A congressional caucus hearing room at the Capitol in Washington, D.C., on October 10.

The event: A quasi-official hearing into the invasion of Kuwait by Saddam Hussein. Congressmen and others are listening to a sobbing, 15-year-old Kuwaiti girl with the assumed name of "Nayirah" describe Iraqi troops taking babies from incubators in the al-Adon Hospital and throwing them onto the floor to die. The press received a media kit, prepared by the Kuwait lobbying group Citizens for a Free Kuwait, containing Nayirah's written testimony. The event is covered in real time on American television with CNN leading the coverage.

The reaction: Three months passed between Nayirah's testimony and the start of the first Gulf War with Iraq. Over the course of those months, no story about Iraq's invasion was repeated for the American television viewer more times than Nayirah's story. President Bush himself recited the story many times in front of Congress, the UN Security Council, and on television and radio. It gave the Kuwait invasion a human focus and helped galvanize public and Congressional opinion as a reason to go war with Iraq. On January 12, the U.S. Senate voted by a narrow five-vote margin to support the Bush administration in a declaration of war.

Postscript: The public relations firm Hill & Knowlton created and organized this part of the Kuwaiti promotional campaign in the United States, trying to get Americans behind the proposition of going to war with Saddam and ejecting him from Kuwait, their client-country. It was later discovered that Nayirah was the daughter of the Kuwaiti ambassador to the United States and that her story could not be verified, even by Amnesty International. CBS's 60 *Minutes* reported that a representative of Middle East Watch, a human rights group, had gone to the hospital and interviewed two doctors who were working at the time of the alleged incident. They said the incident didn't happen.

The year: 1980.

The battleground: The campaign between several Democratic Party candidates to become that party's nominee to run against Ronald Reagan for the presidency of the United States.

The media report: Senator Edward Kennedy's candidacy for the Democratic presidential nomination dissolves after NBC interviews him about the Chappaquiddick River car crash where he survived and his companion,

Mary Jo Kopechne, did not. The popular magazine *Reader's Digest* also features a story on it.

The public reaction: The percentage of people who thought Kennedy lied about the incident *doubled* after these media reports.

EXAMPLES ABOUND

Anecdotes like these abound concerning the effect of the news media—particularly television news—on occurrences in politics, government, and government's foreign policy as well. Some insist the media directly controls and sets the agenda for the government and for politicians. If the media go hot and heavy after a story, the familiar refrain goes, then politicians will be right behind in elevating that issue to the top of their agenda, and racing to be first to draft legislation addressing the issue. Others disagree. How do you know that what we witness is not the government manipulating the media into chasing a particular issue? For example, some observers point to the issue of Mexican immigration and ask why it became such a hot-button issue for the media in 2006, right in the midst of heated debate over the war in Iraq and President Bush's policies in continuing to press that war. Hasn't the problem of Mexican immigration been with us for a long time, these skeptics ask? Why should it surge—seemingly overnight—to near the top of the media agenda in the spring and summer of 2006? Might it have something to do with intentional efforts by aides of President Bush to distract media (and therefore public) attention away from the war in Iraq and onto an issue that—while divisive—is not nearly as politically detrimental to the White House?

If you are tired of all the debate on how powerful the media or the government is in setting the other's agenda, and you want to know who is pulling whose strings, you'll have to wait in line. Often that answer depends on who you ask and what their evidence is. And sometimes, frankly, the answer appears to be that both sides are right. Sometimes the media appear willing or unwitting participants in chasing stories the government wants them to chase; other times politicians find themselves chasing issues that the media has enlarged by its coverage. Over the decades, political scientists, journalists, politicians, and political pundits have put forth many arguments about the media's power in influencing the government and politicians. These arguments range from the often-heard critiques about the "liberal" media, to the less-often-heard critiques about the influence of conservative groups on the mainstream media, to various behavioral theories of media impact, and more.

SOME VARYING THEORIES

We'll begin with a couple familiar refrains often heard about the media and its power over the government and politicians.

The "Eastern Liberal Media Establishment" subtracts from everything positive and decent that Republican administrations try to do. That was the view espoused by deposed Vice President Spiro T. Agnew a couple years before his boss, President Richard Nixon, was brought down, mainly by two young reporters working for the *Washington Post*. Their names were Bob Woodward and Carl Bernstein.

Conservative radio talk show host Rush Limbaugh would have us believe there is an undefined "historic shift" that has taken place in the mainstream media. As he noted on his radio program the day after Election Day on November 3, 2004,

> You have called on and off, worried about the power of the mainstream press. You've worried about the ability of the mainstream press to shape opinion out there, and throughout this period I tried to tell everybody that there's a historical shift taking place in this country, an historical shift not just ideologically between liberals and conservatives, but a historical shift taking place in the media—and last night, all day yesterday, this whole campaign. We've now got the evidence of this. This was a huge, huge sweep.[4]

Others, however, might say that the media's effect on the public is one thing, but that the public (or certain blocs of it) also have a definite effect on what the media reports in the first place. ABC's former anchorman, the late Peter Jennings, believed this constant conservative attack on the mainstream media by Limbaugh and other influential conservatives was taking its toll on what was reported and how it was reported by the networks. Speaking as part of a panel discussion just before the 2004 Democratic Convention, Jennings noted the following:

> I think there is this anxiety in the newsroom and I think it comes in part from the corporate suite. I think that the rise, not merely of the presence of conservative opinion in the country, but the related noise being made in the media by conservative voices these days has had an effect in the corporate suites. And I think it worries people. And I might be dead wrong about you, but I hear more about conservative concern than I did in the past.[5]

At the same panel discussion, CBS's Dan Rather underscored Jennings' concerns about conservative bloc pressure and said:

> They have always been good at it but they've gotten better at it. Now, if you touch one of the most explosive issues that led to this polarization, they have instant response teams that will be all over your telephones, all over your e-mail, all over your mail. Mind you, this is not an indictable offense, this is America and they are entitled to do it. But part of what you have to do in a newsroom now that you didn't have to do before, you might have had to deal with a hundred telephone calls before, now if the orchestrated campaign by either one of the parties or some politician's campaign gets on you, you may have several thousand e-mails and telephone calls to which you have to respond.[6]

Most observers might agree that media pictures work on the emotional jugular of the public who, in turn, create huge, instant demands on the White House to take action. That is the view of *Time* magazine journalist Lance Morrow, who believes media images are "mainlined directly into the democracy's emotional bloodstream without the mediation of conscious thought."[7] Therefore, in China's Tiananmen Square in 1989, when student dissenters built a "Goddess of Liberty" which looked like the U.S. Statue of Liberty and paraded it through the streets of China, the image's effect was unmistakable in the hearts of American viewers. Democracy, American-style, was coming to China. Or at least it would have if these students had their way. No thought was given to how improbable that scenario would have been in 1989 China, but there was that ingrained image which somehow said it was possible.

Stories about political issues that are personalized into identifiable human beings and dramatic anecdotes also move the public emotionally, demanding a governmental response to a crisis that may or may not be a reasonable one. Many scholars in the field of journalism believe that the structure of news stories can have definite effects on the meanings received by the viewers or readers. And the structure that seems to have the biggest effect is that personalized narrative that has become so popular in both electronic and print reporting. Find a person caught up in the issue, someone the reader can identify with who hopefully has attractive familiarity, deliver an extended opening anecdote focusing on this person in the throes of his or her crisis, then move to the larger issue once you have the reader or viewer hooked.

The media focuses attention on the critics of the White House, especially when policy seems to be articulated slowly following a crisis. In such cases, however, the president may just be buying a little time to produce a reasoned response. That drumbeat of criticism which winds up on the evening television news often forces the president to make quicker decisions than he would like.

In psychology, Cognitive Learning Theory says our behavior is largely based on what we know. Today, what we know comes almost entirely from the news media. But since the media gives us only a representation of reality—a kind of shadow world with varying degrees of accuracy—our behavior and reactions may or may not be valid or consistent with what really has transpired.

Critical Cultural Theory suggests that those with the money and the muscle form a cooperative, elite group in government and media. The media set the public agenda, and the role of the media is to mobilize public support for special interests that dominate government and society. Noam Chomsksy, linguistic scholar at the Massachusetts Institute of Technology, was a strong proponent of this theory of how media affect the public. This theory has good support in history, going as far back as the pre-Revolutionary days in colonial America as Samuel Adams, Isaiah Thomas, the Committees on Correspondence, and the Sons of Liberty used the colonial media to stir up passion for going to war with England. This historical example will be detailed later in this book as we look at the role of the media in national development. Another example of this same phenomenon took place during the Administration of Woodrow Wilson prior to the U.S. entry into World War I. Believing America had to get behind this war, President Wilson created a contemporary version of Adams' Committees on Correspondence, called it the Committee on Public Information (CPI), and recruited journalists to organize its pro-war propaganda. The result was one of the most unified times of public opinion in American history as the U.S. entered the war.

In modern times, journalist Ellen Hume quotes President Clinton's former press secretary, Mike McCurry, in noting the balancing effect that media bloggers were having on journalism in the political arena. McCurry said:

> Internet blogging is becoming for the Democrats what talk radio was for the Republicans. The blogosphere is center left. The world of the Internet and electronic activism is not Republican. Two exceptions are the Christian Coalition and the National Rifle Association. But they have not found an Internet voice.[8]

CNN senior analyst Jeff Greenfield, now with CBS, is another great fan of the bloggers, Hume said.

Another possibility is the so-called "CNN Effect," often championed by news executives at the 24-hour Cable News Network following CNN's exclusive live audio coverage of the first bombing of Baghdad in 1991. Essentially, this theory stated that CNN blazed such a path with that coverage that it became a defacto "diplomatic channel," used both by President George Bush and later by Saddam Hussein. This came when CNN's Peter Arnett had exclusive escort by Iraqi troops to targets of American bombing as the only Western reporter to be allowed behind the scenes by Iraq during that war.

This CNN Effect was minimized by British scholar Piers Robinson in his 2002 book, *The CNN Effect: The Myth of News, Foreign Policy, and Intervention*. Looking at crises in the Balkans, northern Turkey, and elsewhere, Robinson concluded that the CNN effect often only speeded up a foreign policy proposals already in the works, as was the case following the infamous marketplace massacre in Sarajevo in 1994. He said President Clinton had already been thinking about U.S. involvement in the Balkans, but that the coverage of this massacre and the public outcry following the coverage only put that policy into high gear.[9]

Still, opinion is divided among many scholars and other observers on just how important an influence the news media are when it comes to national policymaking—especially at the level of entering into wars. As later discussion will point out, researchers tend to follow either an enthusiastic position of media influence, a moderate position of media influence, or a position held by some that the media has very little influence on national policymaking. As the importance of the mass media continues to expand around the world, this latter school of thought becomes smaller and smaller every year.

THE SHRINKING CUSHION OF TIME

One of the first things any journalism student learns, after the importance of accuracy, is the importance of the deadline. It is an ever-present reality in the news business, and it comes at a higher velocity as media technology has made live, real-time news coverage a reality and often a necessity. The media may be live television or it may be the World Wide Web, but speed is of the essence today if journalists wish to be the first to get the story to the public. And being first with an important story is still a chief criterion by which journalists judge their success. The tradition of the deadline, the desire to be first with the story, and the sophisticated media technology have merged to create what I began calling "turbonews" a decade ago. And if news was fast then, consider how much faster it is today. Deadlines have always created tension for journalists who are also pursuing accuracy in their stories. The two entities often do not mix well, as journalists need time to verify information before rushing into print with it. Deadlines have often forced journalists to "go with what they've got," and have forced others to withhold stories from publication or the air in order to insure the accuracy of their information.

But the news deadline does not just affect the journalist; it also affects the newsmakers. In the case of politicians and government officials, the news deadline means they must make a decision on how to respond to issues and incidents requiring their attention. And these same politicians and officials must decide—quickly—how to respond to reporters' questions about real-time events and issues. In short, the cushion of time that government officials enjoy has shrunk considerably, thanks to the speed of media technology. In fact, that time cushion has disappeared entirely in many cases. That is the essence of real-time reporting after all: incidents are reported as they are in the process of occurring. Earlier we outlined some historical incidents that have required a quick government response, and showed how the real-time news media affected those responses, and with what effects.

THE SPECIAL ROLE OF VISUALS

Media guru Marshall McLuhan left us with a legacy of opinion and theories about the role each mass medium assumes in delivering impact as well as information to the reader, viewer, or listener. Among his sometimes-enigmating sayings, which confused many journalists, were his two opinions that "the medium is the message" and the slightly altered (but significantly different in meaning) "the medium is the *massage*." By the first of these, the late Canadian English professor meant that any news or entertainment medium is as important as the message it delivers. It is important because it is not a neutral delivery vehicle—like a Domino's pizza delivery car—but rather has specific characteristics that influences the message being sent. A lot of journalists would agree with this.

Take, for example, the earlier point about story structures and their influence. One of the most used story structures is the common and traditional story format known as the "inverted pyramid." In this format, a story's *conflict* is the focus of a *summary lead* which often polarizes that conflict to make it even more dramatic. The story focuses on the event or issue, and is told in an impersonal style. The *details*—and often mitigating circumstances which would moderate the polarity—are not used until later in the story. Contrast that story format with a narrative format in which the reader is introduced—sometimes painstakingly— to a major character and/or scene in a story, and the reader sees the conflict build slowly and is able to understand its subtleties and different dimensions. Often we are handed different impressions of the same event or issue, simply in the different ways the writer tells the story. If you transfer this point to photojournalism (either still or video photography), you reach the same conclusion. Especially in the world of television journalism, the video drives the written story. A TV journalist writes to the video he or she has. It's as simple as that. If you have a lot of video on one aspect of a story, you tend to write more about that aspect. If you have little or no video on a story, then the story itself is often shrunk from the normal 90 sec- onds it probably would have received, to a 10- or 15-second "reader" on the air.

Of course, by their very nature, visuals cause us to process stories differently. A classic example is the tragedy of 9/11. A person who saw those airliners strike the Twin Towers and then saw the towers crumble before their eyes was affected ("massaged" as McLuhan would say) much differently than if the same person had just read a story about the event or even seen a still photo of it. That is because television not only delivers an account of the experience; it delivers the experience itself, in all its rawness and with all the emotional—and often surreal—impact that live television brings. Much was made of this phenomenon in the 1960s when Vietnam burst into American living rooms on the evening news. Even though that was not live coverage, the visuals of recent (and hereto- fore unseen) events proved too much for Americans to sustain over a period of years. Most observers feel that this coverage led President Nixon to conclude American involvement in Vietnam sooner than he wished. So again, McLuhan's theory on the medium being the massage seems validated. We are shaken up differently by each new medium that comes along.

Today, the World Wide Web only enhances and amplifies television's real- time affect by serving as a depository for so much live and recent video footage from around the world and from so many different sources. Often that footage is more graphic than what viewers see on television news. In the case of 9/11, Internet users could find several sources on the Web that featured photos of individuals leaping to their deaths out of broken windows of the Twin Towers. Those visuals were deemed too graphic for most television networks and stations and were not shown. A person seeing a photo—possibly a close-up—of a human being leaping to certain death to escape the oncoming flames is going to be affected much differently than one reading a story about it or seeing video footage of the Twin Towers without the leaping victims.

Although up to this point we have been talking about the effects of photojournalism on individual viewers, the same point can be made concerning that effect on politicians and government officials. Could it be that government policy is sometimes driven by pictures the media broadcasts? Many would agree that is exactly the case.

Writer David D. Perlmutter does a fine job discussing this effect as well as some disagreement concerning it:

> The idea that a picture can drive political policy and public opinion—the concept of *visual determinism*—is not novel. In the world's first major treatise on governance, Plato's Republic, the philosopher expressed concern about the nefarious effects on public opinion and political decision-making by vivid visual images. Today, many people believe that the "problem" of pictures influencing policy and opinion has hypertrophied in the late twentieth century. The allegation that news images have an especially resonant ability to drive, alter, or overturn foreign policy has received currency and generated controversy since the Vietnam War. Among those who espouse such a belief are presidents, members of the foreign policy establishment, and reputable and influential reporters and pundits. In contrast, most mass communication researchers and some journalists and politicians are quite skeptical about any theory of news that posits strong or powerful effects on viewers regardless of informational context, cultural prejudice, or interpersonal influence. Claims of the powerful effects of pictures in the press, however, are so persistent, and made by such influential and powerful voices in media and the political structure, that they cannot be dismissed merely as hyperbole.[10]

Perlmutter refers to many of the more graphic and revealing photos of journalistic history (e.g. the execution of a Vietnamese prisoner in a Saigon street in 1968, and the lone individual standing in front of a line of tanks in Beijing's Tiananmen Square in 1989) as "icons of outrage" that do, in fact, drive some foreign policy decisions. Perlmutter defines these icons in the following manner:[11]

- *Celebrity*. This does not mean the photo focuses on a celebrity. It means instead that a famous picture is one that most individuals could recall instantly when asked about it, or that they have seen the photo but are not quite sure what the context of the event was.

- *Prominence*. Is the photo used by editors on the front page of the newspaper, the cover of the magazine, or does it lead the first news segment of the evening television newscast?

- *Frequency*. How often is the visual used, either by the news medium that originated the visual, or by others who have picked it up from their network or a news agency? As we know, some of the most important and startling visuals have been shown hundreds of times and are still seen today. The planes crashing into the Twin Towers is one obvious example, and the explosion of the Challenger space shuttle moments after it left its launcher is another.

- *Instantaneousness*. Many of these "icons" become instant celebrities in the world of photojournalism, known by all within a matter of hours sometimes.

- *Transposability*. These icons are easily used by different kinds of media, whether print, broadcast, or the Web.

- *Frame of Subjects*. While not a requirement of an "icon," some of these photos are helped along if there is a celebrity figure framed within the photo. We're not just talking about celebrities from the entertainment world, but also those from the world of politics and government. If a photo contains a well-known person or persons, clearly it will become more instantly recognizable.

- *Importance of events*. Usually, the more significant the event depicted, the more attention the photo is likely to receive.

- *Metonymy*. Photos of certain events are often used to "typify" more general events or conditions. One such photo might be back in Tiananmen Square when youthful Chinese protestors carried a homemade replica of America's Statue of Liberty through the streets. The marchers were advocating democratic reforms and were using the statue as an icon of democracy and freedom. The photo seemed to capture that thought for many who saw it. One way of stating this quality of an icon is simply to say, "A picture is worth a thousand words."

- *Primordiality and/or Cultural Resonance*. About this quality, Perlmutter notes, "When we make allusions to biblical or classical historical scenes related to an icon, we suggest that it taps into some deeper human sensibility. This is not only because such scenes are part of our common cultural history...but also because certain images may call to mind primordial themes."[12]

- *Striking Composition*. Certain photo angles and/or photos captured at just the right moment in history enhance a photo's chances of becoming an icon. One photo that comes to mind is of Babe Ruth's last game at Yankee Stadium. The photo, which won a Pulitzer Prize, shows the Babe from behind as he stands along the baseline acknowledging the standing-room only stadium which forms the landscape of the picture. Most photos of a celebrity would not be shot from behind him or her. This one was and became an icon because of its striking composition.

Although some might disagree that visuals have an arresting affect on government policy and sometimes do drive it, many others would say the evidence over time speaks for itself, both domestically and internationally.

THE TECHNOLOGY FACTOR

The global influence of the news and entertainment organizations has been the result of media expansion and the expansion of technology over the past three decades. For example, a group of Swedish innovators launched Space Media Network (SMN) in 1985 as a vehicle to provide up-to-the-minute photos to television networks and other news organizations. These photos included ship and troop movements, construction of facilities designed to produce nuclear and chemical weaponry, and other items that formerly only government intelligence agencies had access to. As Patrick O'Heffernan notes, the first SMN exclusive was the distribution of some of the first photos of the Russian Chernobyl nuclear reactor disaster. Since that beginning, SMN has located secret preparations for a Soviet space shuttle, a powerful Russian laser installation, resumed Soviet nuclear tests, new cocaine plantations in South America, and so on.[13] Over the past two decades, other news agencies have joined SMN in providing other timely—albeit controversial—photos for news organizations. Certainly, satellite distribution has expanded in offering global coverage heretofore unseen. A picture of what satellite distribution looked like in 1991 was laid out by O'Heffernan in his book, *Mass Media and American Foreign Policy*:

> INTELSAT has grown to global coverage with footprints and downlinks in 170 countries, and has increased its global programming from 1,000 hours per year in 1970 to 20,000–30,000 hours in just the trans-Atlantic market. Regional satellite networks have sprung up, including: AUSSAT in Australia, and CANCOM on Canada which send signals nationwide; ARABSAT which covers 22 Middle East and North African nations; NORDSAT which serves five Scandinavian nations; and ESA which serves eight nations in Western Europe, with EUROSAT soon to link all of Europe simultaneously. [14]

And that was in 1991. Over the past two decades, the satellite distribution system has multiplied and is employed now by such new world media players as Al Jazeera, the Dubai-based, Middle East-oriented news giant, which has recently announced an English-language TV channel in America. Through advanced satellite transmission technology, it and other non-Western news agencies are now beaming their alternative perspectives around the world. No longer is the world getting its views of world news from Western news agencies alone. As Dizard points out, direct broadcast satellites have dramatically expanded the accessibility of 24-hour news and information about every corner of the world. One of these satellites, owned by Rupert Murdoch's News Corp., delivers news and entertainment programs to millions of small earth stations in more than thirty nations ranging from Japan to the Persian Gulf. As this transmission occurs, he notes, White House and State Department officers scramble to respond to what are often "superficial sound bite reports of complex events."[15]

On the receiving end of these global satellite transmissions are millions of wireless laptops, cell phones, PDAs, and other handheld devices that mean those who can afford to do it can stay up to the minute with their knowledge and understanding of real-time governmental and political issues and events. Sometimes the public learns about something just as government officials learn about it themselves. Often journalists learn about these events *before* the politicians do. When you take intrepid and enterprising journalism and match it with global satellite distribution technology, you have the recipe for forcing government officials and politicians to respond to events and issues as they are unfolding. You shrink the cushion of time these officials used to have in analyzing and responding to issues, and often there is no cushion at all. When the public hears about something they deem important in the world, they want a response from the White House or Congress, and they want it as soon as possible. Attempts to delay that response in the interest of making sense of it first are often seen as efforts at obfuscation. And then the media will report about *that* public reaction, pressuring the government officials even more to respond.

SUMMARY

These and other views on the media's influence abound, and this book will attempt to detail many of these arguments and provide examples of how the various theories of media impact on government play out in real life. Some of the above points will be analyzed again in other settings and contexts. Research has a lot to say about how the media affect the government and politics, and vice versa. History abounds in examples of how the media and the government interface, both in times of peace and in times of war.

CHAPTER 2

The Media and Political Action

If elected officials care about staying in office past the next election, then they care deeply about the kind of media coverage they receive. And one thing is certain about elected officials: they do care about staying in office. The democratic system of government in an open society places great influence—implied though it may be—on the news and entertainment media. What kinds of stories, events, and people do these media focus on? Looking just at the entertainment media for a moment, let us take a look at just a few motion pictures in recent and not-so-recent history.

MEDIA, POLITICS IN FILM

Many Americans put a lot of trust—perhaps too much at times—in films with political themes that develop viewpoints or conclusions on issues affecting the nation's security and/or its general welfare. Of course, these conclusions are often based on card-stacking (which is one of the critiques often heard of Michael Moore films like *Bowling for Columbine* or *Farenheit 9/11)* where all evidence supporting the producer's conclusions is highlighted, and evidence detracting from that conclusion is omitted or downplayed. Sometimes this is done in the interest of enhancing the dramatic narrative rather than for propaganda purposes. Either way, however, the result is often something less than a balanced look at a what is often a very complicated political issue.

Some examples of films that spotlight the relationship between the media and political action are the following:

- *All the King's Men* (1949 and 2006), about corruption in the governor's office and the entire political process in Louisiana.
- *Man of the Year* (2006). In this satire, actor Robin Williams plays a Jon Stewart-type political comedian who, on a lark, runs for president of the United States. In a massive computer glitch, he is handed the election, although in reality receiving only 16 percent of the vote.
- *The Constant Gardener* (2005), about a conspiracy between the British government and a major pharmaceutical company which results in many deaths in Africa, including that of a western journalist.
- *Good Night and Good Luck* (2005), about the confrontation between Sen. Joseph McCarthy of Wisconsin and CBS newsman Edward R. Murrow over the issue of communists in America.
- *Syriana* (2005), a complicated mixture of stories about competing interests and methods involving oil in the Middle East.
- *The Manchurian Candidate* (1964 and 2004), about the political brainwashing of prisoners of war, one of whom becomes a candidate for vice president of the United States and runs into attempts to control him politically.
- *Veronica Guerin* (2003), about an intrepid Irish journalist who paid the ultimate price for investigative reporting.
- *Thirteen Days* (2000), about the Cuban missile crisis that threatened war between the United States and Russia, and how President John F. Kennedy handled it.
- *Primary Colors* (1998), a fictionalized look at President Bill Clinton's first bid to become president of the United States and the compromises that were made along the road to the White House.
- *Wag the Dog* (1997), about the staging of a fake war by a political consultant to take the heat away from a disastrous character flaw of the man seeking re-election as president.
- *JFK* (1991), about a far-reaching conspiracy between government, business, and organized crime which resulted in the assassination of President John F. Kennedy.
- *Mississippi Burning* (1988), about the murder of three civil rights workers in Mississippi and the attempted cover-up of the crimes by local government authorities.
- *Missing* (1982), about a government cover-up of the murder of a social worker in a Central American country.
- *The Year of Living Dangerously* (1982), about a clash of reporting orientations in covering an alien culture.
- *All the President's Men* (1976), about the Watergate break-in and massive cover-up efforts by top officials in the Nixon White House.
- *Mr. Smith Goes to Washington* (1939), about a naïve junior senator who struggles to remain true to his principles in a maze of political corruption in Washington, D.C.

For Hollywood, stories about political intrigue and the sometimes-corrupt policies of federal and state governments have long been a favorite subject matter for films. And, to the movie going public who have flocked to the above films and bought DVDs of them later, the government is also a fascinating subject.

DEPICTIONS IN PRINT

In the world of non-fiction books, a staple topic has always been the government, elected officials, and the often wayward and/or chaotic nature of the federal government, especially in times of crisis. *Living History*, a political and personal memoir by Hillary Rodham Clinton, was an immediate hit when it was published in 2003, and President Bill Clinton's 957-page *My Life* was a best-seller before it was even published in June 2004. It led the parade of a dozen other successful politically-driven books that year, including books by political satirists and pundits like Al Franken and Bill O'Reilly. In December of 2005, the popular online bookseller Amazon.com showed 53,760 current book titles dealing with the keyword "politics," which was more titles than any other single topic on the Amazon Web site.

As for daily journalism, the political beat is the ultimate job to which most reporters aspire. To become a political columnist in a newspaper is synonymous with success, and becoming a White House correspondent is the dream of most television journalists. Listen as a veteran *Washington Post* political columnist, Richard Cohen, describes how he feels about his job:

> I see myself as the reader's proxy, lucky enough by virtue of occupation to go where they cannot go. I can visit places they're not likely to go and under conditions they would probably avoid (the Middle East almost a dozen times, Africa, Central America, Asia and Europe over and over again) and, sometimes most perilously, the halls of Congress or the salons of Georgetown. I've covered every presidential campaign since 1968 and still can't understand why the primary season doesn't start in Florida or Arizona and wind up in Iowa and New Hampshire. Most days I cannot wait to get to work. I love what I do—the reporting, the writing, the thinking, the constant exploration. Sometimes I think I have the best job in the world. Some days I think Tiger Woods does. But at least I work in air conditioning.[1]

As later chapters will detail, political journalists are the favored few at many publications, and politics is the beat many print journalists aspire to. Additionally, some of the most highly regarded publications—among them *The New Republic* and *The Nation*—are politically focused and are regular reading for many of the highest officeholders in America. In a democracy that prides itself on open elections, those candidates running for office (and the shows they stage in their campaigns) are seen as some of the most intriguing and important reading by many Americans.

TELEVISION COVERAGE

In television journalism, national politics is deemed one of the most important—
if not the most important—story, especially within a year of a presidential election. Count the number of public affairs and "talking heads" programs that focus
mostly on politics and the workings of government. Just at the national level are
shows including the following:

- *Face the Nation*
- *Hannity and Colmes*
- *Lou Dobbs Tonight*
- *Meet the Press*
- *Nightline*
- *The O'Reilly Factor*
- *The Situation Room*
- *This Week*
- *Washington Week*

And these are in addition to the regular network and cable nightly news
programs that focus most heavily on national and international news. Almost
any national story can be seen as having political dimensions to it, because
of the number of laws and regulatory activity that government officials super-
vise. Like their print counterparts, television reporters aspire to the coverage
of high-profile political campaigns and—once the candidates take office—to
the coverage of the officeholders, the policies they enact, and the slips
they make. A later chapter in this book will analyze the relationship and the
dynamics existing between television journalists and politicians. One thing
that is changing in the media landscape of political coverage is the way in
which some of that news is being reported in an effort to draw in different kinds
of viewers who have turned away from the traditional channels of political
news.

POLITICAL COVERAGE, MTV-STYLE

As the media continue to evolve and younger voters lose interest in the traditional forms of political coverage on television and in print, newer forms of coverage take their place. Perhaps none is more radical than what the cable
network, MTV, did in its coverage of the 2004 presidential election. Speaking
to the younger generations in America, MTV has emerged as more than just a
venue for music videos. Using the common thread of music to reach young
people, MTV began incorporating news and political coverage into its menu of
options for its viewers several years ago. In a way, MTV has picked up on the

formula that made *Rolling Stone* magazine so successful: reaching out to younger generations through music to also deliver political news and commentary, and doing it in a decidedly unconventional style. MTV tried two different strategies to reach young viewers with news about politics in 2004. The strategies focused on the different types of correspondents it employed to interview politicians and deliver the news. Among its "correspondents" was hip-hop music artist P Diddy, who had an important on-screen role as a part of the network's coverage of the 2004 election. Among other things, P Diddy reported from the floor of the Democratic National Convention where he interviewed the likes of Jesse Jackson and Sen. Hillary Rodham Clinton.

MTV decided to move unconventionally into political news coverage because of the statistics showing most 18- to 24-year-olds are avoiding news coverage from traditional print and broadcast venues. The Pew Center found in 2002 that this age group spent nearly 40 percent less time with the news than their predecessors before 1994. For those between the ages of 25–29, there was a smaller, but still substantial, decrease of 23 percent for the same years.[2] As for political news, a 2004 Pew study found that people between the ages of 18–29 are showing only minimal interest in political news, at least from traditional sources. Only 23 percent of people in that age group reported that they "regularly learn something" from network news.[3]

Instead, researcher Geoffrey Baym noted, in an insightful 2006 study, that political comedians like Jon Stewart have stepped into the vacuum and have taken young viewers' attention away from the traditional network news anchor. Baym explains:

> ...Comedian Jon Stewart has become an important voice in the landscape of broadcast news. Indeed, at the start of the 2004 presidential campaign, Newsday named Stewart as the single most important newscaster in the country, ahead of Tom Brokaw, Dan Rather, Tim Russert, and every other network newscaster. It is not surprising that Brokaw and Rather's age and style rendered them irrelevant in the eyes of many young people...As young people continue to turn away from news, the entire issue of credibility—of journalistic authority—is now in play in profound ways. Bill Moyers recognized the point in an (2003 PBS) interview with Jon Stewart. "When I report the news on this broadcast," Moyers said, "people say I'm making it up. When you make it up, they say you're telling the truth. For many, the traditional newscaster has lost credibility, but the comedian speaks truth."[4]

MTV delivered its coverage of the 2004 campaign with its *Choose or Lose* series, which was composed of several news reports from both national party conventions and additional half-hour and hour-long programs that covered the presidential race and attendant issues from many different perspectives. Among its correspondents were the following:

- Gideon Yago, a 26-year-old white man who anchored MTV's news coverage. To some degree, he approaches the style of more traditional news anchors on the networks, "positioning himself as the representative of the institution of broadcast journalism," according to Baym.[5] He came across to the viewers as a knowledgeable news reporter in the traditional paradigm. There are departures with traditionalism, however, as Yago also positions himself as a representative of young Americans, speaking in their vernacular and wearing dress common to his generation.

- Sway, a young African American reporter who is also a bridge between MTV's entertainment and news sides. By his name alone, Sway distances himself from traditional network newscasters, and he goes further than that with his presentational style. His role is to speak for young African Americans.

- Christina Aguilera, who seemed to draw her authority as a celebrity from the fact she was covering issues related to sex, and who, by her own admission, knows something about that. So, as Baym notes, she draws her authority from her personal familiarity.

- Drew Barrymore, the actress with even wider name recognition, whose claim to authority is her celebrity status but also that she asserts she is representing the "politically disaffected youth."[6]

- P Diddy, the popular rap music artist, who rounds out the Choose or Lose list of correspondents. As Baym notes, at times he is the "subject of the coverage, primarily for his get-out-the-vote advocacy. He also, however, functions as a reporter at the party conventions and hosts and narrates the program *Hip Hop Politics*."[7] Clearly, P Diddy serves as a representative not just for young people, but specifically for the younger demographics of urban minorities.

So these are the correspondents and commentators that MTV fielded in its coverage of the 2004 presidential election, and it remains to be seen how far down this unconventional path future coverage will travel. Such coverage is controversial within the journalistic community, but it also has been proven to reach the viewers who have tuned out the traditional coverage. In that, it has promise.

THE WEB AND POLITICS

With each of the four major television networks making a decision in 2005 to begin offering first-run episodes of popular shows on the World Wide Web, it is no surprise that political candidates are also moving their campaigns online. This second front (candidates still use television as a major platform) is becoming a very effective means of reaching especially the younger voters, much as MTV is doing. Some of the advantages of the Web over television are obvious. For one, campaigning on a candidate's Web site is much, much cheaper than campaigning on television, where advertising costs are so expensive. Another advantage is the multimedia platform that the Web offers, where candidates can mix text, video, and audio on the same media platform.

The importance of the World Wide Web cannot be underestimated when it comes to the way politicians run their campaigns in the twenty-first century. Individuals seeking their party nominations have always made their initial candidacy announcements in press conferences for the traditional news media of newspapers and television. However, when Hillary Clinton announced her candidacy for the Democratic nomination for president in the winter of 2007, she chose to make her announcement on her Web site, www.hillaryclinton.com. The same thing occurred when New Mexico Governor Bill Richardson made his announcement for the Democratic nomination on his Web site, www.richardsonforpresident. com. Richardson's Web site also contains links to other aspects of his campaign, which are featured on MySpace, Facebook, YouTube, Zanby, PartyBuilder, and Flickr. Richardson has a presence on all of these sites with interactive blogs.

The question that many observers have about political Web sites and blogs, however, is whether these sites actually recruit any voters from other camps or whether the main users of these sites are voters already committed to that candidate and/or party. Are Hillary Clinton and Bill Richardson speaking mainly to other Democrats on their Web sites? If so, that can be effective as they work for the party's nomination, but less effective when it comes to general elections when campaigners hope to snare crossover voters from other parties.

If this is true with politicians, it is likely true with campaign issues as well. When it comes to controversial issues like stem-cell research, gay marriage, or the war in Iraq, people seem more likely to go to blogs if they already have a passion about that issue; then they would likely go to the blogs that support or reinforce their positions on the debatable issues. Basic communication research in the selective perceptual processes (exposure, attention, and recall) would indicate this is true.

Another use of the Web by political candidates and parties is to air the mistakes of opposing candidates. Every national candidate—and many state candidates—have operatives with video cameras (or at least cell-phones) follow opposing candidates on the campaign trail. Often these operatives are waiting for the candidate to slip up, or to find them in an embarrassing public moment. When it happens, the moment goes on the video disk and is quickly uploaded to YouTube, Facebook, and MySpace. Such moments occurred, for example, when Howard Dean went into his rant following his poor showing in the Iowa Caucus for the 2004 presidential election.

ABC's *Nightline* focused on the Web as a new venue for political mudslinging on November 2, 2006. Martin Bashir noted that four days before the national midterm elections, the Internet had become a vital force for mudslinging and trickery. YouTube.com, Myspace.com, and Facebook.com have been favorite sites for such mudslinging. Any candidate or group can put up whatever videos they like, showing such things as candidates falling asleep at important meetings, or Sen. John Kerry's verbal slip on Oct. 31, 2006, in suggesting that those who fought in Iraq were there because they didn't get a good enough education. Another site is Wikipedia.com, where anyone can contribute to encyclopedic definitions of people, issues, groups, or causes. If a candidate wants to contribute to the profile of an opponent, and maybe refer to an "addiction" that this person has, it can be done. The fact that Wikipedia is a favorite reference site for Internet users means false impressions may be handed out to unsuspecting readers.

BLOGGERS IMPORTANT

Chapter 1 introduced the subject of political bloggers, and it is an important area of discussion. As more and more news consumers have turned to the Internet for their information and commentary—and a chance to exchange views with others on political issues and candidates—Web logs (blogs) have expanded the frontiers of political coverage. A quick check of a Yahoo.com listing of political blogs in late 2005 revealed 383, like the following:

- Wonkette—online roundup of gossip from Washington, D.C., and the U.S. political arena from Ana Marie Cox.
- InstaPundit—commentary on politics, science, and culture by Glenn Reynolds.
- Andrew Sullivan—independent journalist provides a daily dish, and links to some of his more controversial pieces.
- Daily Kos—political analysis and other daily rants on the state of the nation.
- Talking Points Memo—political discussion by Joshua Micah Marshall.
- Free Republic—gathering place for independent, grassroots conservatism on the Web.
- Democratic Underground—daily missives against George W. Bush.
- Baghdad Burning—blog from Iraq, talking about war, politics, and occupation.
- Power Line—weblog from two lawyers, John H. Hinderaker and Paul Mirengoff, and attorney Scott W. Johnson.
- Juan Cole: Informed Comment—thoughts on the Middle East, history, Islam, and religion by Juan Cole, Professor of History at the University of Michigan.
- TalkLeft—liberal coverage of crime-related political and injustice.
- WatchBlog—2004 election news, opinion, and commentary covering Republican, Democrat, and third party perspectives.
- Small Victory, A—weblog by a woman who stands by her convictions with a fierce determination.
- USS Clueless—voyages of a restless mind. A weblog by Steven Den Best.
- Turning the Tide—official weblog of Noam Chomsky, including exclusive, original observations drawn from personal correspondence, ZNet Sustainer Forums posts, and direct blog entries.
- Blogs for Bush—group blog dedicated to helping George W. Bush get re-elected as President of the United States in 2004.
- Liberal Oasis—where the left is right, and the right is wrong.

And these blogs are in addition to the countless numbers of politically-sponsored Web sites hawking candidates and political ideologies at every level of government and for every conceivable political party, splinter group, interest group, or political action committee.

IN THE SPOTLIGHT

In short, elected officials, their performance, and their utterances are in the spotlight night after night, week after week, month after month. They are under the media microscope, and the results are beamed back to their constituents— and political enemies—every day of the week. Even if they are not national political celebrities, their local media back home are focusing on their daily performance. So a senator from Oklahoma, while possibly not grabbing the national spotlight, is the focus of political commentary in metropolitan daily newspapers like the *Oklahoman* and *Tulsa World* that his or her constituents and opponents read. With so much constant coverage, is there any doubt that elected officials are concerned with their images and let that coverage influence the kinds of legislation they propose and the way they vote on important issues?

Here is one blogger who thinks that congressional votes are predicated on how much coverage the media is giving a particular issue, and what those journalists are saying about it:

A blogger writing on the Web log *Alabama Improper* (www.alabamaimproper. blogspot.com) noted the following in November 2005 about two of her state's senators:

> Don't tell me the media don't influence the politicians of our time; shame on them. Two of Alabama's finest Republicans come down on opposite sides of a debate that took place regarding the White House regularly reporting on the progress of the U.S. mission in Iraq and a strategy for bringing U.S. troops home. Senator Richard Shelby, R-Tuscaloosa, voted for the resolution. However, Senator Jeff Sessions of Mobile at first voted for the resolution but then changed his vote to "no." The next day he explained why:
> "I got to thinking about it and talked to some other senators and I didn't like it. I felt like it would be spun as it has been in the *New York Times* and the *Washington Post* as some sort of negative resolution. So I decided to vote against it."[8]

A HIDDEN DISEASE?

Some observers have noted that the connections between politics and media form a kind of hidden disease that has infected the American democratic political process. What they are talking about is the fact that media companies are often among the largest contributors to political campaigns, yet it is rare that they cover their own connection with financing these campaigns. From January 1995 to June 1998, media companies (not even including telecoms) gave almost $31 million to the campaigns of federal political candidates. And, writes

Sheila Kaplan in *Columbia Journalism Review*, they appear to have gotten their money's worth.

> From the government giveaway of up to $70 billion worth of broadcast-spectrum space, to protection of lucrative tobacco ads in newspapers and magazines, to fending off competition for ad dollars from the postal service's foray into direct mail, to dodging free airtime for political candidates, to avoiding taxes on Internet services, the media lobbies have enjoyed enviable success.[9]

Additionally, political advertising—money paid to the media by political campaigns—is the single highest campaign expense for any candidate running for a state or national office. Political analysts in the year 2000 estimated that federal and state candidates would spend $600 million on political commercials that year. According to Paul Taylor of the Alliance for Better Campaigns, that's just one turn of a self-perpetuating cycle that is damaging democracy. Costly commercial time and ad space in print media means candidates must raise major stockpiles of cash. But large donations and sophisticated campaign ads create cynicism towards politics, which causes viewership and readership to lag. Disinterest by voters means low ratings for political coverage, which is cut back, prompting candidates to buy more TV ads. And the cycle goes on and on.[10]

President Bill Clinton once noted that the United States is the only major democracy that doesn't require the media to offer free air time for political parties or candidates. Vice President Gore formed a commission in 1997 to look into the possibility of granting national political candidates five minutes of free air time each night for the 30 days leading up to the election. CBS President Leslie Moonves chaired that commission and seemed in support of the proposal, which the commission endorsed. But the proposal received very little attention in the news media, and it was largely ignored by most major media, including Moonves's own CBS.

As for radio, in 1981 the Federal Communications Commission eliminated most public-interest requirements for radio stations and then awarded hundreds of new licenses under the assumption that competition would foster diversity and quality in the radio marketplace. But the 1996 Telecommunications Act all but made diversity disappear entirely, as stations were allowed to merge into larger and larger national conglomerates. Former FCC Chairman Reed Hundt and FCC Chief of Staff Blair Levin expressed concern that the FCC had vacated its oversight of public-interest radio.[11]

To be sure, the candidates do get such free air time in the form of news programs and interview shows, but the control of those programs is largely out of their hands. Not totally out of their hands, because so many political candidates hire former journalists to advise them on how to wrest control of the journalistic interview away from the reporter asking the questions. And some of these candidates have gotten very good at doing just that.

24-HOUR NEWS NETWORKS

A key development fueling the media focus on political action has been the rise and popularity of 24-hour cable news networks like CNN, Fox News Channel, and MSNBC. All of these networks mix news, interviews, and political commentary into their daily programming day and night. Another 24-hour player is C-SPAN, the unique, no-nonsense daily video journal of some of the key proceedings of Congress and of various other government agencies. C-SPAN also covers conventions of the Society of Professional Journalists and the American Society of Newspaper Editors to see what the other half of Washington's power equation—the news media—are thinking and reporting. C-SPAN is a private, non-profit company, created in 1979 by the cable television industry as a public service. Its mission is to provide public access to the political process. C-SPAN receives no government funding; operations are funded by fees paid by cable and satellite affiliates who carry C-SPAN programming.

According to the Project for Excellence in Journalism in 2005, the three nightly newscasts have seen ratings decline by 34 percent in the past decade, nearly 44 percent since 1980, and 59 percent from their peak in 1969. The best evidence suggests it is availability of the half-hour nightly shows, rather than content, that is hurting evening news, but there seems little opportunity to change that. In contrast, news and commentary shows are in abundance throughout the day and night on the cable news channels. By 1999, Pew data was showing cable with a 13-point advantage over ABC, NBC, and CBS combined. In March of 2003, the gap had widened to 27 percentage points. The obvious question is why this should be. After all, ABC, NBC, and CBS all have long histories of producing quality news programs. Is cable news that much better? The answer, as alluded to earlier, is that it is not the superior quality of cable news that is drawing audiences away from the networks. In fact, in that half-hour evening time slot when network news programs are on at the same time cable news is, national audiences prefer the broadcast networks. And that preference shows strongly in the evening ratings. The Project for Excellence in Journalism notes, "This suggests that people apparently do not prefer the way cable does the news; they prefer its instant availability. The age of appointment news – when people would structure their time to wait for a certain program to come on—has faded. People now want their news, or their kids' programming, or their cooking show, when they want it."[12]

COMMENTATOR POPULARITY

Actually, the popularity of individual cable journalists/commentators like Anderson Cooper, Lou Dobbs, and Bill O'Reilly suggests strongly that more and more Americans prefer the way cable television does news. And the way that cable was doing that in 2005–2006 has relevance to the topic of the media's influence on government action. That style, as evidenced by the above-noted cable journalists, is being called various things, from "emotional journalism," to "passionate journalism," to "personality journalism," to "opinion journalism," to just flat-out editorializing. One of the obvious differences between cable news programs is that, while network newscasts appear under the names of "NBC Nightly News," "CBS Evening News," and ABC's "World News Tonight," cable news programs are titled for their news personalitites. So we have Fox's "Special Report with Brit Hume," and "Fox Report with Shepard Smith." CNN has "Lou Dobbs Tonight," and "Anderson Cooper 360" (also known as "AC 360") in addition to the many commentary shows featuring everyone from Geraldo Rivera, to Hannity and Colmes, to Bill O'Reilly.[13]

Cooper was the subject of an entire hour-long Larry King Live in June 2006, wherein King pressed the intense Cooper on his emotional brand of journalism. "Most reporters stand on the sidelines and watch," King noted. "You get angry. Why?" To this, Cooper responded that he hopes he is never rude but that sometimes he believes showing anger at a politician or government official is the only way to get a truthful answer instead of just a "response."[14] Cooper said he "made a promise" to the people of New Orleans to keep covering the story until it was all told. It's obvious he sees himself as articulating the frustration of victims who have no public voice.

It may be the latest evolution in subjective journalism, but the brand of emotional journalism practiced by such television commentators as Anderson Cooper and Lou Dobbs do add another aspect to the way in which the media influence politicians and spur them on to action.

IN COMPETITION WITH CELEBRITIES

In the final analysis, all politicians, including the president of the United States, are in competition with myriad other celebrities and hot-button events for attention of the television cameras, and, hence, the American public. Journalist Howard Kurtz has written about this in his book, Spin Control, as he spoke of the importance to the administration of live television coverage surrounding the president's annual State of the Union Message. In 1996, as he began his second term, President Clinton knew he needed to be seen in a positive light by the American people, and he figured his State of the Union message was the venue for that positive media attention. It is an annual spotlight every president uses to make his agenda known for the year and to make his case for that agenda. The problem, in 1996, was that on the very night of the State of the Union Address, the television networks were awaiting another huge story: the return of the verdict in the O.J. Simpson wrongful death civil case in Santa Monica, California. It was believed the verdict was imminent and would fall on that January evening. Kurtz describes what happened this way:

It was nothing short of remarkable; Here was the president's big ceremonial moment, the House chamber packed with lawmakers and Supreme Court justices and dignitaries of every stripe. Yet Rather, Jennings, and Brokaw were all blathering on all evening about the imminent Simpson verdict, essentially blowing off the president. At 8:10 p.m. [Press Secretary Mike] McCurry called Robin Sproul, ABC's Washington bureau chief, who was coordinating the pool coverage for the networks... "I want to know if I'm going to see the president of the United States in a little box with O.J. filling up the screen," he said. Next, McCurry put together a conference call with Sproul and the bureau chiefs from CBS, NBC, CNN, and Fox "The president is going to deliver the State of the Union to Congress at nine o'clock. It's a responsibility we take very seriously. I hope you'll all do the right thing." An awkward feeling hung in the air... "the ball's in your court," he said. He wanted to put pressure on them to make the proper journalistic decision, O.J. or no O.J. Some truths were self-evident, he felt It was not the time for a harangue by the press secretary. You simply didn't upstage the president of the United States during his annual address to the nation.[15]

As it turned out, the issue was moot since the O.J. verdict was not forthcoming until just after the president finished his hour-long State of the Union Address. Nevertheless, the coverage of that verdict did subtract mightily from the post-Address commentary on television, and it won headlines in the nation's newspapers the next day.

In increasing numbers, national political candidates are choosing to join the celebrity ranks rather than trying to outdo them with their own moments on television. So, in February of 2007, both former New York City Mayor Rudolph Giuliani and U.S. Senator John McCain made their presidential campaign announcements for the first time—at least informally—on two popular evening talk shows. Giuliani made his initial campaign announcement to seek the Republican nomination for president on Larry King Live, while McCain told David Letterman that he would run for the same nomination. Knowing both Democrats and Republicans watch these shows, and that both shows do well in the ratings, these and other candidates are obviously finding this to be a good venue for making major announcements.

POLITICAL ACTION COMMITTEES

No discussion of the media and politics would be complete without talking about the role of the political action committee (PAC) in the election process. These committees, formed for myriad special interests in America (and, in some sense at least, all interests are special interests), are huge supporters of political candidates and ballot issues. A quick Internet search yields an encyclopedic list of the different PACs that exist, or at least those that are known. Yet despite their importance to the election process in America, PACs themselves may not get much media coverage. Possibly that is because there is no human face or identifiable visual image to a PAC. It is an organization, and organizations don't draw much in the way of media coverage without an identifiable face to show on screen as the leader.

In a generic sense, PACs and their special interest groups are often publicly derided by politicians running for office. The irony is, however, that most of these same "reform-minded" politicians are also receiving money for their campaigns from PACs. It would seem that to these politicians, some special interests are more justified in connecting with than are others. And the "others" are usually the ones supporting the opposing candidate(s) or issue.

It is interesting that the National Association of Broadcasters (NAB), representing many media companies, also contributes to PACs and is itself a kind of PAC, a very real lobbying influence in the nation's capital.

In any event, a 1999 Harris Poll of just over 1,000 adults found that 83 percent of the public believes the PACs have become too powerful of an influence on Washington and favor strong support for congressional campaign finance reform when it comes to the activities of the PACs. An interesting additional finding to that same survey showed that 81 percent of the respondents believed that the news media have too much power and influence among lawmakers in Washington. Those percentages were up slightly from an identical survey done in 1994, and an additional question revealed that 54 percent of the public felt that TV/radio talk shows and their hosts wield too much political influence.[16]

An excellent Web site that looks at the activities of various political action committees, especially in relation to their support of different candidates and issues, is found at www.fecinfo.com. This site is called Political Money Line, is updated daily, and is a part of the Congressional Quarterly (www.cqpolitics.com).

SUMMARY

Politics is a big media story in America. It is also a major focus of many Hollywood films, and many magazines are built around political themes. In the American democracy, who the voters have as candidates and how they respond to those groomed and carefully attuned images is big news. Part of the allure of the political story is the theatre of politics itself, rife with drama—and often with scandal and corruption. It is seldom boring, except in the case of unexceptional candidates or issues, but political parties try to insure that the drama stays alive. In a day and age where the Internet has become so popular and has changed our ritualistic ways of obtaining news and entertainment, political handlers have adopted it to their advantage and are now using it as a major venue for their messages about their candidates. Additionally, nontraditional "news programs" such as the comedic Jon Stewart and Bill Maher shows (along with Oprah, Jay Leno, and David Letterman) have changed the way in which many Americans get their views on the candidates and issues facing them. The next decade promises to be very interesting, as the means of unveiling America's political stories to the public continue to evolve in ways the nation's forefathers never dreamed of.

CHAPTER 3

The Media and National Development

Part of any discussion involving the role of the media's influence on government and politics is this question: what role has the media played historically in the development not only of the American government but also governments around the world? And a related question to that is this: are there any discernible patterns revealed by such a study? This chapter looks at the roles the media play in the development of a nation.

THE MEDIA AS AGITATORS

Scholar John C. Merrill believes the media serve a number of roles in the development and maintenance of any nation, and that one of these is the role of agitator.

When we examine the world media today, we get the feeling that the jangled nerves of the world's populations can hardly be eased by the newspapers—and certainly not by TV. On the contrary, anxieties are created, magnified, and perpetuated; religion is set against religion, social class against social class, race against race, and nationality against nationality. Instead of being conveyors of enlightenment and harmony, the national media systems tend too often to be mere extensions of factional and party differences and animosities, thus doing a good job of increasing irritations and suspicions among groups and governments and giving distorted pictures of various nations.[1]

Certainly this is one role that is hard to deny. In any society, journalists are seen as a rather unruly lot who are capable of breaking embarrassing news stories before politicians have a chance to put their own spin on those events. Further, journalists are prone to focusing on the conflict and differences between ideologies, organized groups or parties, and individuals. It is the main reason many governments around the world attempt to put restraints on their media, and some of those restraints are very tight indeed. As Merrill points out in his voluminous writings on international media, some media add their own ideological slants to the messages they deliver to the public, and this only seems to be increasing. "There have been few truces in global psychological warfare," Merrill writes. "As technology pushes mass messages into the more remote regions and saturates ever-growing populations, the world's psychosis is bound to worsen."[2] He adds that even truthful messages offer no guarantee of enlightening or stabilizing individual recipients of those messages.

History abounds with examples that even accurate statements can have a backlash and appear as something completely different if the recipient is from another culture or has another set of values or beliefs than the message's encoder. This takes us into the world of communication theory, of course, and the models from Wilbur Schramm and others that dissect the communication process. Most of these models clearly point out that one of the difficulties with mass communication is that message intended does not always equal message received, and that this may not be the fault of the message itself. Rather, it may be because of the vast differences in perspectives represented among the decoders of the message or those individuals on its receiving end. Truth, philosophers and mass communication scholars might say, is in the eye or ear of the beholder. Nowhere is this more true than when a diverse audience decodes a mass-mediated message. Think of just one example of this: a reporter for Al-Jazeera may believe he/she is laying out a factual message in a news report, only to find that American or Western European receivers of that message perceive it totally differently, partly because of what may be an inherent mistrust of Middle Eastern journalists.

Merrill concludes his thesis by noting, "Worldwide envy, resentment, suspicion, and hatred build emotional walls against the most objective and well-intentioned printed word and erect mental jamming stations against the most honest broadcast."[3]

THE MEDIA AND THE AMERICAN EXPERIMENT

History shows that the genesis for America itself is found in an agitated group of writers, impatient for freedom and separation from the controlling forces of England. Ideas were in circulation long before—and during—the colonial days of America in the work of such Englishmen as John Milton, John Trenchard, Thomas Gordon, Richard Steele, and Joseph Addison. Later, American colonial writers like Thomas Paine, Samuel Adams, and Benjamin Franklin contributed their inspiration. Before there was an American nation, there were the stirrings of early-day poets, essayists, pamphleteers, and journalists such as these men.

If one were to look for articulation of the freedom of expression, one of America's driving forces, he or she would find it in the writings of John Milton. Milton wrote about the freedom to express oneself during a civil war in England from 1642–1649. It was a conflict that pitted the Puritans, under the leadership of Oliver Cromwell, against the followers of the Stuarts and James's successor, Charles I. Although this was a time of bloodshed and revolt in England, it also produced several years of relaxation for writers who found freedom to express their views because of the need for both sides to gain public support. The feared and repressive secret court known as the Star Chamber had been dissolved in 1641 by the Parliament, and voices began to rise for greater freedom of expression. One of those voices was the poet Milton who, on November 24, 1644, published his famous *Areopagitica*. It is one of the most articulate and best-known calls for freedom of the press ever written. Among its famous and often-quoted passages are:

> ...though all the winds of doctrine were let loose to play upon the earth, so truth be in the field, we do injuriously by licensing and prohibiting to misdoubt her strength. Let her [truth] and falsehood grapple; who ever knew truth put to the worse in a free and open encounter?[4]

Milton brought attention to the issue with the phrase, "He who kills a man kills a reasonable creature...he who kills a book kills reason itself."[5]

Although Milton's words had little immediate effect on the rise of the Commonwealth under Cromwell, his ideas were disseminated in the decades to come, and fell upon receptive ears among those expatriates who traveled to colonize America. His *Areopagitica* and other works like it helped form the philosophical spine of those colonials seeking greater freedoms in the young America. It was among the earliest cases of a writer using a mass medium (books) to influence public policy and bring about a change in government.

In the eighteenth century, many voices were being raised in England for the kinds of freedoms that Milton had espoused a century earlier. Among the best of these so-called "essay papers," which were devoured by students on both sides of the Atlantic, were the *Tatler* (1709-1711) and the *Spectator* (1711-12 and 1714). These papers were written by Richard Steele and later both Steele and Joseph Addison. The *Spectator,* a one-page essay sheet, was published daily and sold for a penny. At one time its circulation reached 60,000 readers and was hugely popular. Even more importantly, its literary form was widely imitated in America by Benjamin Franklin.[6] Some of Steel's ideas for his *Tatler* series may well have come from a man regarded by many historians as the greatest English journalist of the period, Daniel Defoe, who was editor of *Mist's Journal* (1717-1720). Some consider Defoe to be the founder of the modern editorial, and he, too, was copied by many pre-revolutionary writers in America.[7]

Another influential series of essays were the ones that were called the *Cato Letters*, written by John Trenchard and Thomas Gordon using the pen name "Cato." This series was published from 1720-23 in the London Journal, which was later called the British Journal. In a convincing and articulate fashion, this series discussed theories of liberty, representative government, and freedom of the press.[8] They, too, were sometimes copied by American journalists who spread their ideas far and wide among colonial Americans seeking liberty.

Chief among colonial American voices disseminated via the printing press that had dramatic influences on the course of the Revolution was Samuel Adams. Adams was one of a growing group of colonials in the mid-eighteenth century who was totally frustrated with England's grip on America, and he decided to do something about it. He organized a group of fellow revolutionaries who would write about the ill effects of colonial subservience to British authority. These essays would then be printed and disseminated throughout the colonies and hopefully give rise to revolution. The following is an excerpt of one of Adams' many written reports:

> The measures of the British administration of the colonies are still as disgusting and odious to the inhabitants of this respectable metropolis (Boston) as they ever have been, and I will venture to add that nothing can convey a more unjust idea of the spirit of the true American than to suppose he would compliment, much less make an adulating address, to any person sent here to trample on the rights of this country.[9]

In the years prior to America's Revolutionary War, Adams was concerned that the colonists may have lacked the determination to endure a protracted fight for independence. So, to help strengthen their resolve, he organized the Committees of Correspondence to spread incendiary messages about the British occupational troops stationed in the colonies. The written reports from these colonial patriots were structured in a carefully worded manner. It was a style formalized by Adams himself, who once called himself "an anonymous manipulator of man, events, and nations."[10] Historians Edwin and Michael Emery said of him, "Sam Adams was not only the propagandist of the revolution, but he was the greatest of them all. He was truly the 'master of puppets' and 'assassin of reputations' as his enemies dubbed him."[11]

The form of argument used by Adams was based on several propositions, including:

1. Advertising the ultimate rewards of victory while minimizing the risks that defeat would bring.
2. Neutralizing any opposing thoughts, regardless of how logical they might be.
3. Phrasing all issues concerning independence in black and white, right and wrong, patriot and British. There could be no room for middle ground nor gradations of viewpoints to distract prospective converts to the patriots' cause.

Among other legacies, Adams' argument style left an irony in American history: those who would cry loudest for independence and human rights would be the same individuals who would deny others the same liberties. Because there were only two ways to view the issue of independence from England, and because only one view (the patriots') was right and virtuous, the Tory viewpoint must be evil and full of danger. As a result, Tory publishers in the colonies such as the philosophical moderate James Rivington found their newspapers put to the torch by zealous patriots who followed the lead of Samuel Adams.

An even more permanent legacy of Adams' propaganda technique is the confining vantage point it puts on issues. Semanticists such as the late S.I. Hayakawa refer to this kind of two-sided presentation as "two-valued logic." It is a kind of two-valued orientation to both language and issues. When it is used consciously, it is an intentional way of simplifying issues that are, in reality, much more complicated. Such simplification can and often does cause distortion, but it serves the writer's purpose.

Adams did not originate this orientation, and it certainly did not end with his writings. The patriot was actually borrowing the technique from such earlier writers as John Milton, author of *Areopagitica*, discussed earlier. Milton used this two-valued logic in his treatise for freedom of expression when he argued for allowing all opinions to have their day in the arena. The truest of them would survive, while the weaker would perish in battle.

Adams was only one of a number of colonial writers who spurred Americans into waging the war for independence. Other patriots were journalist Isaiah Thomas, who published the well-named newspaper, the *Massachusetts Spy*; also Benjamin Edes, John Gill, and Thomas Paine. Together this band of tireless writers and editors created a drumbeat of alleged atrocities attributed to occupying British forces. It was a drumbeat that arose to a crescendo in the hearts and minds of the colonists, which eventually resulted in the first shots fired against the British troops at Lexington and Concord and didn't end until the Revolutionary War was over. Before the war began, patriot writers like Paine urged the colonists to fight by laying down passionate pleas in his *Common Sense* essays. Six months later, the patriots delivered the Declaration of Independence. Once the war began, Paine urged the patriots to stay the course through his *Crisis* papers, which carried such pleas as the famous, "These are the times that try men's souls. The summer soldier and the sunshine patriot will, in this crisis, shrink from the service of his country; but he that stands it NOW, deserves the love and thanks of man and woman."[12]

In assessing the role of the colonial press in colonial America's march toward independence, it is difficult to understate the influence of the writers and newspaper editors of the era. Although published on primitive presses and distributed via slow and primitive delivery methods, over time the essays and newspapers created common thinking among the isolated colonies, knit Americans together, and enflamed them with the passion needed to rise up in revolution against England and win the ultimate victory.

Following the Revolutionary War, America's new Constitution featured a First Amendment mandating a free press, and the Supreme Court has validated its principles—chiefly banning prior restrains—in the twentieth century.

THE EXPERIENCE OF OTHER NATIONS

America's experience has also proven to be true in other countries as well. The equation appears to be that whenever freedom of expression breaks out in a country, that nation is on the road to greater freedoms itself. Certainly that was true in England as the domination of the monarchies began to crumble and, in search for public support, reigning monarchs began allowing more press freedom. Ultimately, freedom of the press began to flourish in England and, with it, a parliamentary democracy took hold for good. Conversely, in countries that refuse to allow a free press, authoritarian governments are the order of the day.

Researchers Siebert, Peterson, and Schramm, and many others, have looked at the different forms of press-and-government relationships in various countries and developed models that help to show how that relationship works. The Siebert/Peterson/Schramm Model, traditionally called The Four Theories of the Press,[13] shows four different systems have been—and continue to be—at work in the world:

1. The Authoritarian System.
2. The Libertarian System.
3. The Social Responsibility System.
4. The Soviet-Communistic System.

Each of these systems works in the following ways:

Under the *Authoritarian System* of press-government relationships, the government allows little, if any, press freedom. The news media often must disseminate information only with the consent of the government, as was the case in colonial America when newspapers were required to publish with permission of English authorities. This theory was developed in England during the sixteenth and seventeenth centuries when monarchical rule was at its zenith. The rationale for this model of press/government relationship is that the media should exist to support and advance the policies of the government in power and to help stabilize the society in the way the ruling powers feel it should be stabilized.

Ownership of the media under this system can be either private or government owned, but if it is private the owners may have to receive permission from the government to publish or air news broadcasts. In some countries, the ownership model is mixed: the government owns the broadcast outlets while private individuals or companies own the print media.

Although the oldest of the theories of press freedom (or lack of it), the Authoritarian System survives today and is in use (to one degree or another) by a great number of countries in the world still under repressive regimes. These are found mostly in the developing nations of the world but also in China. More will be said later about them and the role they have played in the debate over the so-called New World Information Order.

The Libertarian System is in many ways the opposite of the Authoritarian System, for it espouses great individual freedoms for the media. This system was adopted in England after 1688, as well as in the United States during and after the Revolutionary War, and it is influential today in many countries of the world, most notably in Scandinavia. The purpose of this system is for the media to inform, entertain, sell, discover the truth, and serve as a check on government. Ownership under this system is mainly private.

Libertarians believe men and women are rational and can separate the truth of a situation from its falsehood. Thus, they are capable of choosing the true and rejecting the false. We are all capable of determining our own destiny, and we will make the right choices if we are given the right information. If this sounds like Jeffersonian democracy, that's exactly what it is. America's third president believed that if men and women exercised reason, then the majority would make sound decisions as a group, even if some individual citizens may not. Advocates of press freedom often invoke Jefferson's famous line, "Were it left to me to decide whether we should have government without newspapers or newspapers without government, I should not hesitate for a moment to prefer the latter. But I should mean that every man should receive those papers and be capable of reading them."

The Social Responsibility System advocates press freedom but cautions journalists that freedom should not equate with license to print what one wants, without regard to the effect it might have on others. Although most social responsibility systems do not approve of prior restraint (suppressing publication), they do approve of secondary measures (such as libel and invasion of privacy laws) to keep the media responsible in its charge of informing the public while minimizing harm to the innocents.

This Social Responsibility System is the one historically practiced in the United States. Its purposes are similar to the libertarian goals (inform, entertain, sell, and serve as a check on government), but it adds another purpose: to raise conflict to the plane of discussion. Ownership under this system is chiefly private.

This theory is an outgrowth of libertarian theory, although most observers would agree the notion of social responsibility theory goes beyond "objective" reporting to "interpretive" reporting. The idea of presenting a larger picture of events, putting issues into context, and pursuing truth as well as the accuracy of individual facts, are all parts of this theory. It is a theory that had its formal birthing with the Commission on the Freedom of the Press. The commission studied the freedom and accountability of the press. It was formed in 1947 by Robert Maynard Hutchins, president and later chancellor of the University of

Chicago, with the financial support of *Time Magazine* founder Henry Luce. Over its history, the commission produced several reports. It was sometimes known as the (Robert) Hutchins Commission. In part, the commission stated in its reports:

> It is no longer enough to report the fact truthfully. It is now necessary to report the truth about the fact...The emerging theory does not deny the rationality of man, although it puts far less confidence in it than the libertarian theory, but it does seem to deny that man is innately motivated to search for truth and to accept it as his guide. Under the social responsibility theory, man is viewed not so much irrational as lethargic. He is capable of using his reason but he is loath to do so.[14]

The overall urging of this commission was to have the media conform to a social responsibility approach and provide the following:

1. A truthful, comprehensive, and intelligent account of the day's events in a context which gives them meaning.
2. A forum for the exchange of comment and criticism.
3. The projection of a representative picture of the constituent groups in society.
4. The presentation and clarification of the goals and norms in society.
5. Full access to the day's intelligence.

One of the reasons this theory of media operation was deemed important is because of the growing power of the elite media in the United States and the near-monopoly position of many corporate media giants. Because the media have become such a huge industry, the thought was that its executives could use a little urging to insure their news and information products do, in fact, serve society in a positive manner.

To find validation of the Hutchins Commission's findings, one has only to look at the codes of ethics adopted and revised over the years by groups such as the Society of Professional Journalists and the American Society of Newspaper Editors. The latter group's Canons of Journalism call upon newspapers to practice responsibility to the general welfare, sincerity, truthfulness, impartiality, fair play, decency, and respect for the individual's privacy.

The fourth system in the Four Theories of the Press Model is the *Soviet Communistic system*, which was obviously developed in the former Soviet Union, although parts of it were put into place by the German Third Reich in the run-up to World War II. The purpose of the media under this system is to contribute to the success and maintenance of the Soviet socialist system, and especially to the dictatorship of the Communist Party. Ownership is chiefly public under this system. Even though the Soviet Union no longer exists, Communism does, most notably in China. And communist countries still believe in the main tenets of this system, the chief one being upholding the values of the Communist Party.

Since China occupies so much of the world's attention today and accounts for such a large percentage of its population, it is interesting to look at how that nation's media system has developed and what the relationship is to the development of the media system in that country. In fact, China just recently made a big change in its media policy, tightening an already restrictive policy on the international dissemination of news about that country and its government.

The Chinese experience is one where the controls on the media reflect the country's normal relation to its people and other institutions: repression and censorship.

Although many political scientists perceive the People's Republic of China (PRC) as a communist state, it is also the richest of such states. Additionally, efforts to define China's political structure into just one category are often perceived as shallow characterizations. Throughout much of Chinese history, the country has been ruled by some form of centralized imperial monarchy. This has usually been followed by a chaotic succession of mostly authoritarian Chinese National governments and administrations ruled by warlords since the last few years of the Qing Dynasty in 1912. Even though the PRC regime has been portrayed as authoritarian, communist, or socialist, signs are that the country appears to be moving toward a capitalistic economy. Nevertheless, the government does repress liberties in many sectors, most obviously in the traditional and newer media forms such as the Internet.

China is ruled for the most part by the Communist Party of China (CPC), although there are other political parties allowed. The country generically refers to these as "democratic parties," although the name is something of a misnomer. These parties contribute to the People's Political Consultative Conference, although—in reality—their role is to support policies of the Communist Party. The party maintains control over all major governmental appointments. There is, in fact, no real opposition, and the CPC wins elections by default in most jurisdictions. To add to its power and authority, the CPC has been tightening its grip on all political dissidents. At the same time, the party has tried to improve economic conditions and even permit public expression of personal complaints just as long as they don't become organized protests. Whether the CPC has the support of the general electorate is impossible to detect, inasmuch as there are very few elections that are actually contested.

The Chinese government's relation to the media mirrors its relation to its people. While on the surface the CPC appears to grant liberties to the media, a simple scratching of the surface reveals a repressive system. Like other former communist empires such as the Soviet Union, China's constitution guarantees freedom of speech and freedom of the press. Its operational definitions of these phrases, however, falls short of the idea that Western democracies have of them. The government practices open censorship of political speech, and the media is routinely censored in the so-called interests of national security. The Chinese government believes in suppressing most protests and institutions that it feels may threaten the stability and unity of the nation. Such was the case in 1989 when student protests broke out in Tiananmen Square and were greeted with a government response that included many arrests and tanks in the street.

The government's control of the media is not complete, however, as courageous journalists and media organizations have printed or aired stories that expose social problems. Some media also take on government corruption, which is a dangerous thing to do in China. The door for such wildcat media actions has been opened by growing public outrage over the CPC's repressive policies. In a situation similar to the lax British enforcement of colonial American newspapers, the Chinese government often finds itself in such need of public support that they permit some disagreement of their policies in the media. But this is not a systematic policy, and censorship is more the order of the day. In an indication of where China stands worldwide in regard to media freedoms, the organization Reporters Without Borders in 2005 ranked China 159th out of 167 countries in degree of press freedoms allowed.[15]

In its 2006 Annual Report, Reporters Without Borders assessed the state of censorship by the Chinese government as it noted the following:

> Faced with growing social unrest, the government has chosen to impose a news blackout. The press has been forced into self-censorship, the Internet purged and foreign media kept at a distance. Every day, Chinese editors receive a list of banned subjects from the Propaganda Department, renamed the Publicity Department. These include demonstrations by peasants, the unemployed or Tibetans—nothing escapes the censors who stoke up a climate of fear within editorial offices. When the army opened fire on villagers in December, draconian measures were put in place: The press was banned from carrying anything but reports from the official Xinhua news agency, foreign reporters were persona non grata in the region and every reference to the village was erased from the Internet.[16]

This last reference to the Internet refers to a September 2006 policy that China instituted to censor foreign news coming into their country and to reinforce the monopoly control of China's official news agency, Xinhua. The new policy, which China says is just an extension of its 1996 media policy, places editorial control over the distribution of foreign news agency content in China within the hands of Xinhua editors. The new policy extends to weblog entries and affects U.S. Internet service providers such as Microsoft, Google, and Yahoo. Weblog entries on some parts of Micosoft's MSN site in China using words such as "freedom," "democracy," and "demonstration" are being blocked, as well as phrases like "human rights" and "Taiwan independence." China is using a system called Night Crawler to patrol the blogs, and all Chinese bloggers are required to register first with the government before starting their online journals.

On the other end of the world spectrum from huge countries like China, one finds small countries like the satellite nations that once—along with Russia— formed the Soviet Union. One such country is the Baltic State of Latvia. A country that gained its independence from Russia only in 1991, it is today savoring its newfound freedoms. Chief among those is freedom of the press, and any journalist visiting Latvia will tell you how excited the Latvian journalists are about having the freedom to report and write what they believe to be true, and to investigate issues of corruption in the government. *Diena*, the country's largest daily; *LTV*, the country's leading television station; and the new information/opinion magazine *Republika* are all staffed with journalists who have freedom to help move the country toward pluralism and democratic reforms. Such freedoms were virtually unknown less than two decades ago under the Soviet laws regarding press freedom. And such freedom is allowing the entire country of Latvia to remain free of despotic control as the numbers of political parties and philosophies continue to gain strength and attract followers among the people.

Contrast that with life under the Communist Party where, as one Republika staff member said in a room full of other staff members in June 2006, "All of us here can remember when it was illegal to express any objections to what the government was doing. Many of us have family members or friends who were taken in the middle of the night and sent to Siberia, and some have never returned." This comment came as this author interacted with many Latvian journalists who all echoed the same feelings and evidenced the same excitement about life as free journalists. Clearly, free governments and free media go hand in hand and form a symbiotic bond that strengthens each other's freedoms.

THIRD WORLD EXPERIMENTS

Governments of developing nations around the world often follow a pattern associated with seeking greater stability, which often translates as tighter government control over its institutions and people. Usually the scenario has played out where a new government comes into power on the back of a military coup, restricting general freedoms in the process until the new group gains a measure of stability. Sometimes that stability never occurs, and always the first institution (other than any opposing military forces) taken over is the nation's mass media center. Considered by some as a developing nation, Thailand is the most recent case study of this scenario. The 2006 Thailand coup occurred on September 19 when the Royal Thai Army rose up against the government of Prime Minister Thaksin Shinawatra. It was the first coup in that country in 15 years, and took place only a few weeks before the regular elections were slated. The Army cancelled the planned elections and did what other such coups usually do: issued orders suppressing and censoring the mass media, suspended the country's constitution, eliminated Parliament, and outlawed all organized resistance and protests. Although the coup was a bloodless one, its result was nevertheless effective in installing the military in control.

The Army used the head of public relations for Thailand's Channel 5 to make the announcement of the coup at 11 p.m. and to ask for public cooperation with the new government, which began calling itself the Council for Democratic Reform. One of the first measures of the CDR was to remove foreign television news channels like CNN, the BBC World, Bloomberg Television, and CNBC from the air. National Thai broadcasting stations were still allowed to remain on the air from Bangkok. On the second day of the coup, the CDR officials demanded that the country's mass media cooperate with the new government and its policies. They also instructed the minister of Information and Communication Technology to ensure that his ministry monitored all media stories and commentary, and censored those deemed negative toward the new provisional government.

Such is the normal pattern of developing nations, and such is the philosophy that these governments use for taking control of the country's mass media. It is deemed necessary for provisional stability. The problem is that "provisional" time stretches out to years or even decades and—often in the interim—another coup takes place and another provisional government steps in to take control of the media. The process is perpetuated, and neither the media nor the country have a chance to breathe the air of freedom for very long, if at all.

Another reason given for taking control of especially the foreign media is this: the governments of these nations believe there is an unequal flow of international news and information, and that most of it originates from unfriendly Western nations who misunderstand the Third World regions and carry disinformation to the people of these countries. This was the basis of the plea by several developing nations' delegations to the Sixteenth Session of the United Nation's General Conference of UNESCO, in November 1970. UNESCO is the United Nations Educational, Scientific, and Cultural Organization, and among its areas of interest is the way the news media impact countries and the approaches they take to the stories they distribute. The delegations, led by India, proposed several reforms, including establishing international communications networks and helping insure cultural autonomy of nations (presumably, in part, by lessening the incoming flow of values from other cultures which often are part of media programs or stories.)

At the next General Conference of UNESCO, the focus shifted to satellite transmissions of media programs via DBS or direct broadcast satellites. The Soviet delegation was leading the charge on this debate, insisting that a declaration be approved that endorsed the idea of "prior consent" when dealing with DBS programming transmissions into a country. The resulting resolution (No. 2916) was approved by the Seventeenth General Assembly of the United Nations by a surprising vote of 102 to 1. The United States cast the lone opposing vote. Then the Soviets proposed another resolution that focused on what they called "fundamental principles governing the use of the mass media." Again, the U.S. dissented and said such resolutions would have the opposite effect of what they were purportedly designed to do, and would instead cut off the free flow of information that already existed in the world. Eventually, the chief resolution approved became known as the New World Information and Communication Order.

A few years later, in 1978, the United Nations established a Commission for the Study of Communication Problems and named Sean MacBride, the Irish Ambassador and head of Amnesty International, to chair it. It became known as the MacBride Commission and released first a controversial interim report, creating concern over the nature of the Western media and—in particular—the wire services such as Associated Press and United Press International. It suggested a proposal for countries to intervene via their governments, possibly by issuing licenses to journalists operating in those countries. It was not greeted warmly by Western delegations. The MacBride Commission produced its final report in 1980, and most felt it was a compromise meant to satisfy the West in watering down the verbiage used to describe the Western media. Also, the report suggested that industrialized countries provide subsidies to developing countries instead of having countries issue stringent demands on information flow. In sum, there were more than eighty recommendations made in the report which concluded with "the setting up of a new world information and communication order."[17] The report also rejected the notion of licensing journalists, and proposed a resolution focusing on "professional integrity and standards." Chief among the ideas expressed in that phrase were that journalists be allowed freedom to report but that they exercise responsibility and professional ethics in doing so.

The debate over the shape of the New World Information and Communication order continued for several years (and, in fact, still continues today). However, there came a point in 1984 when the United States, under the Reagan Administration, believed UNESCO had moved too far afield in trying to dictate educational, social, and cultural policies that were too anti-Western in their nature. Secretary of State George Schultz concluded the U.S. would apply its resources to "other means of cooperation"[18] rather than UNESCO. The U.S. thus withdrew from UNESCO. In part, the reason that was given was this:

> We understand that there was some progress—perhaps because this is where the United States has concentrated its fire power—and this movement was recognized in review. However, the basic problems still exist, and, even in the communication area, UNESCO's program of seminars and studies still contains the potential for developments hostile to a free press.[19]

In their book, *Global Glasnost*, Johan Galtung and Richard C. Vincent note the following in explanation of the U.S. withdrawal from UNESCO:

> American conservatives were already against many facets of UNESCO long before the Communication Order Debate was formalized. Communication issues calling for a free international flow of information, and guaranteeing all the "right to communicate," just helped highlight many of the reservations they already had about United Nations' operations. But by addressing the licensing of journalists, "assigning them 'responsibilities,'" and monitoring their output," notes Sussman, UNESCO lost esteem among "the influential American press," too.[20]

And then the authors cite the liberal magazine *The Nation* in addressing a *New York Times* editorial. In part, *The Nation*'s journalist wrote, "The odd thing...is that such a licensing system exists in the United States, similarly impairing its freedom...the only difference being that in the United States the orthodox media are trusted by the government to maintain and police the system informally..."[21]

Years have passed since the high point of the debate occurred over the New World Information and Communication Order, and that debate has subsided greatly. In fact, no one seems to be sure what that Order is all about these days, and the whole issue of the dominance of Western news agencies and its wire services has faded as new media distribution forms (and the establishment of regional media like Al Jazeera) have helped equalize the international playing field. The United States has returned to the UNESCO fold, and developing nations still go through the cycle delineated earlier in the Thailand example. Galtung and Vincent suggest that the following could occur for the NWICO:[22]

- There will be better news rations for the Third World—meaning more news about the Third World in the First World and less about the First World in the Third.

- There will be increased Third World control over communication assets—control over which events news personnel from the First World are permitted to extract from the Third World and process into news, and local control over local media.

- There will be more news about other Third World countries in all Third World media and less about the First World.

- There will be some Third World control in the First World over what events should be processed into news, and increased Third World control over local media.

- There will be some Third World control over world communication institutions, including U.N. agencies in the field, if established.

SUMMARY

It is clear, from the histories of individual countries and governments, as well as from the time spent on the issue by agencies such as UNESCO, that a country's mass media have a powerful effect on the way that country grows and develops. There may be no other single institution that has such a pervasive and long-lasting effect on a country, its government, and its people than the mass media. Armies may march in and carry out coups that result in new governments, but other armies are probably not that far behind, and other coups are inevitable. It is significant, however, that one of the first things these armies do when taking over a country is to subdue and claim control of the nation's mass media center. They know the power of that institution, or they wouldn't wrest control of it so quickly. This policy is not only followed by Third World armies but also armies of advanced nations. The American forces employed the policy when they staged their first attack on Baghdad in 1991, targeting the city's main broadcast distribution tower and reducing it to a pile of twisted steel. History shows the validity of this equation: a country's freedoms will develop only insofar as its press freedoms do, and vice versa. This symbiotic influence and relationship between a government and its media seems undeniable when looking at the history of nations.

Chapter 4

How Events and Issues Become News

News stories are representations of reality. They are not reality in and of themselves. As representations, they have certain qualities about them including the following:

1. They are ideas conceived by their creators.
2. They are written in a structure or format designed to suit their purpose.
3. They are written in a vernacular that is appropriate for a large and diverse audience.
4. They come closest to reality when they are accurate in fact and context.

Clearly, not all events, issues, or people find their way into the pages of a newspaper or air as part of a television newscast. There is a selection process that takes place in deciding which of the many candidates for news stories, on any given day, are selected to be written about or photographed. That selection process is implemented by one of several gatekeepers. It could be the assignment editor who schedules the event for coverage; it could be the reporter who decides how to do the story and which parts to emphasize; it could be the sources who decide what to tell the reporter, how to tell it, and what to withhold; or it could be the producer or the city editor who decides whether the finished story is worth airing or publishing. The way events and issues become news is the focus of this chapter.

TRADITIONAL CRITERIA OF NEWS VALUE

When editors or producers start the daily process of deciding what's news, they either consciously or subconsciously base their decision on a number of criteria of news value. The more traditional of these criteria are as follows:

- *Timeliness.* In the news business, time is of the essence. Events that impact a media market and which have occurred within the current news cycle are deemed most important. When newspapers dominated as the public's information source, that news cycle was defined as the portion of the day since the publication of the last issue of the paper. Newspapers continue to use the same kind of news cycle (except in the case of their online editions), but for television the news cycle has shrunk greatly, thanks to real-time reporting brought about by live transmission technology. The same is true for the Web. So timeliness today can be defined as anything happening right now for TV and the Web, to the past several hours for newspapers.

- *Proximity.* This criterion is both geographical, in the sense that events which happen closer to home usually receive more coverage, and psychological, in the sense that events and issues that occur elsewhere yet impact those at home can receive strong coverage as well. An example of the latter would be a farm bill passed in Washington, D.C., which might get front-page placement in a small Iowa daily because of the intense agrarian interests of the farmers who live and work there.

- *Market Conditions.* Closely related to the concept of psychological proximity is the criterion of market conditions. Each media market has its own interests, and the readers and viewers of these markets are often asked by the media what they would like to see featured in the newspapers or on the newscasts. Television has used market research for years, and newspapers have been using it more in recent years to gauge whether their mix of news and editorial content fits their market very well. This concept, sometimes called, *marketing the news*, is controversial in the media (probably more so in the newspaper industry, where reporters aren't as accustomed to it as in television). But it has also emerged as a necessity and as another criterion on which to judge news value.

- *Uniqueness.* When events, people, and issues are unique, they tend to get more coverage. This is one reason why stories about things going as planned and people doing what is expected of them just don't get much coverage. It's also one of the most often-heard criticisms of the news media when people say, "You reporters never cover the good things that are happening!" This criterion is often used in connection with the next one: conflict.

- *Conflict.* The very nature of a news story is conflict, just as it is at the heart of any narrative story either in the news or entertainment media. Without some type of conflict, there is no story. Conflict is what increases the interest of the reader or viewer; what raises the stakes for those characters in a story. It can be overt conflict, such as two men engaged in a fight, or it can be covert, as when two ideologies clash. The challenge for most journalists is to present this conflict in an arresting way, yet keep it in balance and show what may be its many sides.

- *Human Interest.* The technique heralded at most journalistic seminars today is putting a human face on a story, whether it be an event or an issue. It's not a new approach and has been around as long as journalists have written news or feature stories. The more a story lends itself to being told in human terms, the greater play it will receive.

- *The Day's Flow of News.* This is sometimes a criterion of news value that goes overlooked, and yet it is often one of the most important. On any given day, a story may wind up leading the first segment of a newscast or falling to a secondary position in another segment, depending on what it is up against in terms of other stories. By this measure, an event or issue doesn't become newsworthy because of its own intrinsic merits, but rather, because of what else is available in the way of news.

- *The Competition.* This refers not to the competition a story has from other stories, but the competition the news organization has from other media. At times, events or issues are judged newsworthy because the editor or producer knows the competition will be featuring the story, and they feel they must run it, too. It is no coincidence that *Time* and *Newsweek* often feature the same cover story on a given week, even though there may be many candidates for a cover story that week. Media organizations still love to beat the competition. And if they can't beat them, they at least want to stay abreast of them in terms of coverage.

NONTRADITIONAL CRITERIA

There are other ways of looking at the criteria of news value; other ways of defining news. Each culture might have a different definition, to a greater or lesser degree, but in America the news media often draw from the list of traditional criteria and from some nontraditional ones as well. Columbia sociologist Herbert Gans codified some of these criteria in a well-known content analysis he did of some of the elite media outlets in America. His results were published in a book called, *Deciding What's News.*[1] Gans' criteria are actually a pattern of values (which he calls "enduring values") that protruded over time in the media he analyzed. Some surfaced in the patterns of stories covered; some surfaced in the language used to describe people, events, or issues; some surfaced in the sources used for stories. The following is a paraphrased listing of Gans' criteria, or enduring values, which seem to drive a lot of reporting:

- *Ethnocentrism.* This is the viewing of other cultures through the prism of American standards and values, and it surfaces most in foreign reporting. Sometimes countries or cultures become news because their lifestyles or values are perceived as so different from America's. Sometimes they seem to be rated on how closely they conform or diverge from American values and standards. Actually, this is the kind of approach that presidents would like the news media to follow at times. President Bush would have very much liked the news media to judge Iraq as a country badly wanting and needing the kind of democracy he tried to impose in that country. And he would very much like the news media to evaluate the motivation of the insurgents as simply hating freedom.

- *Responsible Capitalism.* American reporters seem to believe that this is a value worth monitoring and, when deviations or threats occur, the event becomes newsworthy.

Corporations are also supposed to be good corporate citizens. Thus, pollution of the environment by a company would be seen as a highly newsworthy story, not only because of this value but because of possible health hazards posed to the community.

- *Altruistic Democracy.* American reporters believe government is to be of the people, by the people, and for the people. Government leaders are to act for the good of the community. Any cases to the contrary, such as using public funds for private purposes, become news.

- *Leadership.* This is closely aligned to altruistic democracy, only it is personified in the character and traits exhibited by candidates voters elect to public office. It goes beyond altruistic democracy in encompassing several leadership traits that are seen as making government officials effective as they carry out their responsibilities. One of those traits is their ability to sell their program to fellow legislators and, sometimes, to the voters themselves. Another leadership trait the media monitors is follow-through. How well does the officeholder carry out the promises that she or he made during the campaign? The 2006 scandal involving Florida Congressman Mark Foley is a classic example of a story built upon the value of leadership and how one leader failed his constituents. Foley resigned abruptly from the House of Representatives when damaging e-mails he had sent young congressional pages surfaced in the media.

- *Order.* This is a big one. It is the basis for so much of the crime news that seems to dominate local television but which also takes up a good part of any newspaper. Crime is the antithesis of—and a real threat to—order, thus it is an important criterion of news value. There are other events and issues that become stories because of order, too. Protests or demonstrations that get out of hand, for example. Or, in recent memory, the chaotic and sometimes deadly evacuation procedures used in New Orleans during Hurricane Katrina.

- *Small-Town Pastoralism.* There is a sense among American reporters that, while the population flocks to the cities, their hearts stay in the country. In many ways, smaller is more valuable, this ethic says. So there is a longing for the simpler ways of small-town America and a belief that this is where life really may be best. There's a sense of nostalgia tied to this criteria; of the way things used to be. So we find stories about the last hand-cranked telephone in a small coastal town of Maine, or the last paddlewheel ferry connecting a small Illinois river town and the City of St. Louis.

- *Moderatism.* Another value that Gans discovered in his study was moderatism; a sense that more value may be found in the center of the stream, rather than on either extreme bank. So when a group or cause gets too radical—such as possibly the Earth First wing of the environmentalists—then they pose a threat to mainstream values and to an earlier value: order. While moderate groups themselves may not get much coverage, the radicals do because of the dramatic ways they often protrude themselves into the public sphere.

- *Rugged Individualism.* Possibly more than any other criterion of news value, rugged individualism is the most important in American journalism. Possibly because America is one of the most individualistic countries in the world, this is a value that journalists seem to prize. So when they see it personified in individual humans (or even animals such as the cougar who defies entrapment by park rangers), this becomes news or at least the focus of a solid feature story. Sometimes individualism may be exhibited by a small group of protestors who fight city hall over an issue. Or even an inanimate object such as an old grain elevator that refuses attempts to be pulled down to make room for a development of new condos. Whenever a reporter finds individualism refusing to bend to group pressure, progress, or the greater odds, there that reporter finds a story.

FEASIBILITY OF COVERAGE

One factor concerning whether an event or issue becomes a news story is this: how accessible is this event or issue to coverage? Many news media don't have the resources to cover the kinds of stories that large dailies or television networks cover. And even the largest of the news operations can find it hard to get access to a story if it is cloaked in national security and/or sources just won't talk. Most issues that involve corruption or illegality are shrouded in secrecy and have built-in layers of protection that discourage serious journalistic snooping. This is true in government, as was seen with the *Washington Post's* 1972 Watergate investigation and more recently with the media probe into the Bush Administration's rationale for going to war with Iraq in 2002. But it is also true in issues involving the private sector. In 1990, the *Indianapolis Star* confronted a code of silence among many in the medical community when that newspaper conducted a probe into medical malpractice in Indiana. Although the newspaper wound up winning a Pulitzer Prize for the eventual series, it took reporters several months of working with sources every day to get the story. Most newspapers don't have the luxury of releasing even one reporter from daily production of news stories in order to spend months probing just one story or one series. So these editors consider such projects unfeasible and rely instead on the Associated Press for the major investigations.

Another aspect of feasibility concerns the possible consequences a news operation faces should it decide to publish or air a story it has gathered. Here we may be talking about some of the largest, as well as the smallest, news media. This concern over consequences is often called the "chilling effect," and it usually focuses on the possibility of a libel suit or other legal action. For example, in the 1990s CBS's venerable news magazine 60 *Minutes* worked hard to secure an exclusive interview with Jeffery Wigand, head of research and development for Brown and Williamson, one of the country's largest makers of cigarettes. The story was dramatized in the movie, *The Insider*, and concerned the practice by the big tobacco companies to make their cigarettes more addictive through a chemical boost process. It is detailed in a later chapter of this book.

Smaller news media face this chilling effect even more than larger media since their financial resources are much less, and the threat of a multimillion dollar lawsuit is enough to bring a chill to some reporting.

Still another aspect of story feasibility is the reporting method that may be required to get the job done. Many news organizations—especially newspapers—have problems with the idea of undercover reporting; of having their reporters assume another identity to infiltrate a group and get a story. The classic example of this came in 1977 when the *Chicago Sun-Times* set up an undercover "sting" operation to catch city officials accepting bribes. The story was successful in drawing attention to widespread corruption in Chicago city government, but the newspaper was denied a Pulitzer Prize and many feel it was because it resorted to undercover reporting to get the story. Most newspapers consider undercover reporting to be a means of last resort and, even then, are loathe to implement it. Television has been more involved in these kinds of "stings," partly because catching a crook in the act makes for good TV. In 2005 and 2006, for example, NBC's Dateline set up several sting operations to lure child predators into a home full of hidden TV cameras, and the program devoted several episodes to this drama. The official rationale for such undercover reporting is that it's necessary to bring a public safety threat to light. Critics of this approach ask: If it's necessary to tell lies to expose lies, is it worth it?

Sometimes this undercover reporting can backfire and lead back to the threat of a lawsuit or even criminal action. When ABC's *20/20* news magazine decided to send journalists into the Food Lion supermarkets to secure jobs and secretly photograph questionable meat packing practices, they wound up with a story, but also with a fraud charge and civil suit filed against them. The case went to a federal appeals court, where the lower court verdict was upheld, but damages were reduced to mere token amounts. But fighting that legal action took a lot of time and a lot of money for the network.

GIFT-WRAPPED STORIES

Another way events and issues become news is by having someone drop the story in a reporter's lap, and clearly this happens a lot in American journalism. Often, stories walk right into the newsroom in the form of individuals who have been through extreme struggles, in the form of special-interest group representatives who have documentation on a threat to public health or safety (and also a threat to their particular cause or movement), or through the form of a political candidate who has documented evidence that his opponent has committed a crime, etc.

The most common form of gift-wrapped story, however, is the government leak. These come both in government-directed leaks and in wildcat leaks that a disgruntled official might reveal in an attempt to embarrass an administration. In the case of a government-directed leak, a designated government official clues a reporter in to a story which is often self-serving and/or damaging to opposition candidates or causes. In the case of a wildcat leak, a government official or bureaucrat takes it upon himself or herself to spring the leak, much as Jeffrey Wigand did as the whistle-blower against Brown and Williamson Co.

Most reporters who cover Washington, D.C., say journalism in the nation's capital would slow down considerably were it not for government leaks. The fact that this term, "leaks," is such a well-recognized and accepted term in Washington, was seen during the Nixon Administration when the infamous "plumbers unit" was established. Its mission: plug the unwanted leaks about the matter known as Watergate and its cover-up. In fact, to a large degree, the plumbers unit was part of that cover-up area.

Sometimes, a gift-wrapped story walks into the newsroom in the form of an individual who the reporter recognizes as a terrific feature subject. Such was the case when a man named Edward Zepp walked into a Florida newsroom and met reporter Madeline Blais, who wound up producing a 1979 Pulitzer Prize-winning feature on this World War I vet on a lifelong quest to replace a dishonorable discharge with an honorable one. The resulting story was called "Zepp's Last Stand."

THE SOCIALIZATION OF JOURNALISTS

Certainly much of a journalist's idea of what is and is not news comes from the socialization process that takes place over time as journalists gather and discuss their craft. A lot of information is exchanged after work as reporters gather for a beer at a local bar (a ritual which seems to have seen better days), or gather at a convention of the Society of Professional Journalists (SPJ), the Radio and Television News Directors Association (RTNDA), or the American Society of Newspaper Editors (ASNE). Additionally, ongoing professional development workshops run by organizations like the Poynter Institute of Media Studies in St. Petersburg, Florida, or the American Press Institute in Reston, Virginia, help inculcate criteria of news value into the minds of reporters and editors. As do other professionals, journalists are often eager to exchange story ideas with others at these gatherings, and especially eager to discuss the successes they've experienced in covering events and issues.

This socialization process is enhanced by at least two other phenomena as well: contests and consultants. The profession of journalism likes to reward those who achieve a certain degree of "excellence" with their stories, editing, and news photography. On the print side, the most prestigious of these awards are the Pulitzer Prizes; on the broadcast side, the Peabody Awards, Dupont/Columbia Awards, and even Emmy Awards are often cited as the most prestigious. But there are many other awards handed out by groups such as the SPJ, RTNDA, and ASNE, for writing, editing, and news photography. Some in the profession feel there may be too much emphasis on these awards, but most seem to appreciate the recognition of a job well done. Along with these awards and award ceremonies, however, comes a growing awareness in the minds of journalists as to what constitutes a good story. Often winning journalists will talk about "how I got that story" or "how I wrote that story and why." This is a very real form of indoctrination, especially for the younger journalists in the audience. A lot of attention is paid especially to the kinds of stories the Pulitzer or Peabody juries notice and make awards for.

Consultants come into play, too, especially for television news operations. Every television station of any size contracts with a consultant like Frank Magid and Associates, or Audience Research and Development, or a host of others. Among the contributions that these consultants are expected to make is to monitor the kinds of news and feature stories garnering large audiences around the country, and to pass that information on to client stations. Some topics become "hot" topics based on the fact that news stations in other markets are chasing and producing these stories and are getting good ratings with them. On the print side, consultants may not be used that much (although readership research is being used more than ever). In the place of consultants, however, some large newspapers will contract for newsroom "coaches," who will coach reporters on everything from the kinds of stories they identify and develop to the writing of these stories.

FOLLOWING THE LEADER

To some degree, some events and issues become news because the elite media chase them first, and other media perceive these stories as news because the industry leaders have so defined them. It's a kind of "status conferral" process that occurs when newspapers like the *New York Times*, *Los Angeles Times*, *Washington Post*, *Philadelphia Inquirer*, *Wall Street Journal*, or *Miami Herald* go hard after a story. Especially in terms of investigative reporting, these are seen as six industry leaders on the newspaper side, as are NBC, ABC, CBS, and CNN on the television side. If these elite news media are on top of an event or issue, others are sure to follow. A classic example was the coverage of Watergate, innovated and spearheaded by the *Washington Post* and *New York Times*, but which eventually captivated media around the country.

Two other media institutions, however, have often been used as the standard-setter; one more by newspapers, and the other more by television. These two media are the Associated Press and *USA Today*.

It is not unusual for a newspaper editor to wonder this about a story one of her/his reporters has just produced: If it is so important, why doesn't AP have it? Of course, part of that answer is that the AP is exactly what its name implies: an association of member news media who are obligated to file their stories with the AP as well as their own newspapers. So the answer to the editor's question might well be: "The AP doesn't have it yet because we haven't given it to them yet!" Nevertheless, the AP does have its own staff of reporters, with bureaus in each large city and around the world. Much of the groundbreaking AP coverage is broken by these wire service staff members. They are good and usually reliable, and newspaper editors around the country know it. In reality, of course, these AP reporters and editors are as vulnerable to making mistakes as any journalist. Over the years, however, the AP has insisted on high standards of accuracy, and their reputation is well-known in the industry. The AP is also unique in that it is the largest wire service, and thus the largest supplier of news to newspapers. The AP has created a thread of unity among newspapers in America and around the world in that the same story done by them may well appear on the front page of newspapers everywhere on the same day. So, absent any other unifying standards in the newspaper industry, the AP has been named that standard, officially or unofficially, by many newspaper editors in America.

In the case of USA Today, while its design influence has had a huge influence on newspapers everywhere, the influence of its content has largely been felt in television. Since USA Today focuses so much on celebrity, pop issues, and trends, many local television stations gravitate to it as a source of some story ideas. If you walk into many television newsrooms around the country, the one paper you will see lying around—in addition to the local metro—will probably be USA Today. Often a local television news crew will try to localize some of the national trends or endless lists (Best Cities/Worst Cities, etc.) that appear with regularity in the pages of this unique national daily newspaper with ubiquitous centers of news rather than the New York or Washington, D.C., centers used by more traditional newspapers.

An interesting experiment in alternative international news is underway with the recent addition to the mix of the Qatar-based Al Jazeera, the multimedia news agency that has grown in such a short time to such great popularity in the Middle East. Whether this independent yet decidedly anti-Westernnews operation will become a standard-setter for U.S. media in looking for news definitions from the Middle East remains a question. In some ways, Al Jazeera already has become just that, as the national media look to it for the latest news about the whereabouts of Osama Bin Laden and other Al Qaeda leaders, and also about the latest reaction of Iraqi and other Middle Eastern countries to the presence of U.S. troops in Iraq and President Bush's efforts to inject democracy into the region. It may become even more of a standard frame-setter for the Middle East, since it announced plans in 2006 to launch an English-language cable television channel in America, staffed with several American journalists.

THE GOVERNMENT AS PUPPETEER

Regardless of how one perceives the issue of agenda-setting, one thing is clear: politicians and government officials spend a great deal of time trying to get the media to turn their issues into news stories, and they often use staged events to bring those issues to the attention of the media and the public. At the federal level alone, the U.S. government is the largest employer of public relations practitioners in America. Cottle and Manning note that in promotional cultures like the U.S., Britain, and Western European countries like Germany and France, political parties are hard at work. The political elites now prioritize the use of marketing, public relations, and advertising techniques in selling politics, politicians, and issues.[2] And, on the reverse side, they put restrictive mechanisms in place that clog up unwanted information flow, much like the plumbers unit alluded to earlier in this chapter. More formal restrictions, like the Official Secrets Act, are in place in Britain than the U.S., but America has its share of information restrictive measures.

Sometimes government officials themselves are the puppets, and their strings are being pulled by larger moneyed interests. The puppet analogy was depicted well in the 1983 critically acclaimed film, *The Year of Living Dangerously*. In this film, a young Australian journalist is posted to his first foreign assignment in 1960s Jakarta, Indonesia. The journalist is befuddled by what he sees when he enters the slums of Asia and turns instead for his stories to the palace where all the other correspondents are gathered, chasing the "official interviews" with government officials. The Australian journalist, Guy Hamilton, is befriended by a photojournalist of mixed ethnicity, Billy Kwan. Hamilton's eyes are opened by Kwan as to what the real story of Jakarta is, beyond the official pronouncements at the palace. In one enigmatic scene, Hamilton goes to Kwan's bungalow, where Billy presents an impromptu puppet show designed to show Hamilton that he should focus on the shadows the puppets cast rather than the puppets themselves. Those shadows are the effects of the government's policies on the people of Indonesia.

In sum, the relationship between reporters and politicians or government leaders is more of a collaboration than an armed engagement. There is the knowledge among both parties that one needs the other; hence, mutual interests act as the engine for the relationship and keep it going during rough times. In many ways, the dance between journalists and politicians is thus a waltz of self-interests. At times, of course, one dancer steps on the other's toes, and then the partner is not always easygoing in his or her response to the toe-stepper. In the end, however, one dancer figures out the other's steps, and collaboration takes the team to the end of the waltz.

In some ways, it is odd that there should be such cooperation—which at times goes to collaboration—at all. After all, the goals of the journalist and the politician would seem to conflict: the journalist wants to enlighten (and draw as many readers or viewers as possible), while the politician wants to persuade and propagandize. Additionally, the unwritten codes of conduct between the two are sometimes unclear, and can cause problems and frustrations to rise. Embargoes placed on stories by government officials and politicians, explanations of off-the-record status (and its many variations of veiled attribution), agreed-upon "coded" answers in which a politician may say "yes" or "no" without really uttering those words—all go together to create potential problems between source and journalists. Much more will be said about this relationship in another chapter. The topic is relevant here, however, inasmuch as a lot of news comes from the mouths of politicians and government leaders who are often spinning it in a precise way to achieve a precise goal.

SUMMARY

As the preceding has shown, events, issues and people become news in a variety of ways. Some of them are determined by the news media, and some are thrust upon the news media either spontaneously or as part of a planned information or disinformation campaign. The latter method is especially true as election time nears. Much run-of-the-mill news, however, is judged by either traditional or nontraditional measures of newsworthiness, and those judgments are made everyday by reporters and editors. In any television newscast or any newspaper there is only so much of a "news hole," and these criteria of news value become important to judging what is included as news, and what goes where. Additionally, the various kinds of socialization a journalist goes through will, over time, influence his or her ideas about which kinds of events, issues, and people should become the focus of news and feature stories.

CHAPTER 5

What the Research Reveals

As the academic field of communication studies has grown over the decades, one of the guiding research questions has been this: What effect do the media have on society? Of all research questions, this may be the broadest, most multifaceted, and most difficult question researchers have ever faced—let alone attempted to resolve.

The reason is that we could be asking any of four separate questions:

1. What kind of effects are to be studied?
2. What kind of media are to be studied?
3. What portion of society is to be studied?
4. How do you design a study that will show not just association, but also causation?

DIFFERENT EFFECTS

There are many different types of effects that can be studied, and any researcher must decide exactly what effects he or she wants to focus upon. What effects are we talking about? Are we talking about *psychological effects* and, if so, what kind? Are we talking about *stimulating effects* and, if so, what kind? Are we talking about *agenda-setting effects*? Possibly *trend-setting effects*? Or what about *framing effects*?

Taking these individually, researchers could study a broad field of psychological effects. They could be looking at the issue of *imposed trauma*, for example, as in the trauma television viewers might experience in watching—in real time—the start of a war. Millions of America did just that as they were sitting down to dinner in January of 1991 and March of 2003, when their television screens began showing them raw, live video of American planes bombing cities in Iraq. In each case, Americans had to juggle the trauma of watching their country go to war as they downed their mashed potatoes. Of course, the most traumatic experience of this type was visited upon Americans on the morning of September 11, 2001, when television delivered the horror of the two hijacked commercial airliners crashing into the twin towers of the World Trade Center. When television and the Internet give us this kind of live programming, they are not just delivering reports of breaking events; they are delivering the raw event itself in all its graphic terror. Clearly, this can have some serious psychological effects on many in the viewing audience.

But psychological effects could also include feelings of *alienation* (as when viewers feel cut out of the decision-making processes the media show their government officials making); feelings of *togetherness* (as when news stories focus on the unity a town displays in rebuilding after a devastating tornado sweeps through); feelings of *sadness* (as when television shows stories of family or personal tragedy); feelings of *jubilation* (as when the news presents stories about the end of a war); and feelings of *fear* (as when we are reminded, often every night, of the dangers we face right in our own cities). These are just a few of the many feelings we might have following the media's portrayal of an event.

But psychological impact is only one type of media effect. We could also identify a large grouping we might call *stimulating effects*. These are effects that can turn our perceptions or feelings into actions. It is important to note that, while the world the news and entertainment media present is only a *representation or portrayal* of the real world (I called it a "shadow world" in a previous book), the actions which people take in response to those representations occur in the *real* world. This is the key reason why those in the media producing these representations must get their portrayals right. If they don't, then the real-world reactions to these false portrayals will be inappropriate responses to what really happened. Some critics of government policy regarding the second war in Iraq also take the media to task for failing to discover before the fact that Saddam Hussein apparently had no weapons of mass destruction, which was the main reason the Bush Administration used in going to war with Iraq in the first place. In fact, journalists like Judith Miller working for esteemed media outlets like the *New York Times* were writing stories—later discovered to be based on faulty sources—that Iraq did have such weapons. So the United States went to war with Iraq a second time, and it was up to the Bush Administration to come up with other reasons later to justify the war they had begun when it was found no WMDs existed in Iraq.

So it is important for the media to be accurate about the news of the day; not just for the sake of their own credibility but because people can be convinced to support government responses on the basis of what they see daily in the news—and even entertainment—media. Don't forget that many Americans don't discern the difference between monologues of David Letterman, opinions of Oprah Winfrey or Dr. Phil, and what comes across the evening news.

POSITIVE AND NEGATIVE REACTIONS

The stimulations that can come from media are not only appropriate or inappropriate actions; they can also be positive or negative actions. An example of a positive action would be a public outpouring of support for an individual, family, town, or entire country caught up in a crisis. Time and again we have seen Americans become so moved by portrayals of tragedy on television that they rush to the stores to buy needed goods for victims and drop checks in the mail to help out with relief efforts. At home this has happened followed tragedies such as 9/11, the Oklahoma City bombing, and Hurricane Katrina. But Americans have also been stirred to positive action over the depiction of famine in Ethiopia in the mid-1980s, and in disaster relief to Sri Lanka when the tsunami struck in 2005.

Sadly, as we know, negative responses also follow media portrayals. A prime example would be when televised violence seems to stimulate real-life violence. Much anecdotal evidence exists to suggest these connections do exist. One instance was the killing of 12 students and a teacher at Columbine High School on April 20, 1999. The two young shooters, Eric Harris and Dylan Klebold, had a history of constant exposure to violent imagery in video games, as well as music and movies. Crime analysts have theorized that the teens' obsession with the media may have caused them to confuse reality and fantasy. Many journalists compared the massacre to a fantasy sequence from the 1995 film *The Basketball Diaries*, in which protagonist Leonardo DiCaprio wears a black trenchcoat and shoots six classmates on his high school campus. Some eyewitnesses at the school likened the shooting spree to scenes from the 1999 film *The Matrix*. Several unsuccessful lawsuits against video game manufacturers were filed as a result by parents of some of the victims.[1]

Of course, the issue of the media and violence has been the focus of many academic and government reports. In October 1985, Surgeon General C. Everett Koop convened a "Surgeon General's Workshop on Violence and Public Health" that studied what he believed to be an epidemic of violence that produced an estimated four million victims each year, most of them children, women, and the elderly. The workshop was especially interested in the contributing role of violent visual images portrayed by the media in fostering violence, as well as with the long-term psychological effects of violence on victims, such as the suspected tendency of victims of violence to become violent themselves.

THE UCLA VIOLENCE STUDY

On the academic side, a major study of television and violence was carried out by researchers at UCLA between 1995 and 1998, looking at the content of broadcasting and cable. Called the Violence Assessment Monitoring Project, the study examined every television series, TV movie, theatrical film, and children's program on network television, plus 24 series from the UPN and WB networks.

It did not analyze news programs, however. Additionally, the UCLA researchers monitored every on-air promotion and advertisement. In sum, 3,000 hours of television content were monitored in a single year for each of the three years of the study. Finally, the researchers studied the top ten videos and a sample of video games found in stores. The study, funded by ABC, CBS, NBC, and Fox, found the greatest concern was over theatrical films shown on TV, although editing helped in reducing some of the violence. Also problematic were promotions for future programs which often compressed several violent scenes which seemed worse without the context. Most disturbing, according to the UCLA study, was the violence in films in theaters, home videos, and on pay cable stations.[2]

Ongoing projects dealing with media and violence are often carried out by researchers at the Annenberg School of Communications at the University of Pennsylvania.

AGENDA-SETTING

Another kind of media effect falls under the often-discussed and researched category of *agenda-setting*. The classical notion is that the media, being one of the most powerful influences in American society, sets the agenda for the government (local, state, federal) to follow. In fact, there has been so much written and discussed about agenda-setting that the concept seems—to many people—to be a fact of life: The media does set the agenda. Period. Yet research indicates this issue is not so clear-cut after all.

For one thing, the media's status with regard to a government's agenda is often discovered to be one of *association*. Media coverage on a story or issue is seen as prefacing government action on the issue. But researchers know that associations do not necessarily equal *causations*. In other words, just because stories appear as associated with government response, it doesn't always follow that the stories caused the government response. Certainly there are several research studies that do show this causation, but the research project must be designed in a way to confirm that causation and not just association. These causation studies are harder to conduct because of the need to isolate and weed out possible contaminating variables—in other words, other possible causes. Simply interpreting association as causation may lead to a kind of chicken-and-egg debate: what actually caused what?

For example, does a media story on immigration problems cause the White House to act on immigration, or was it a well-planned campaign by the White House to get the media to focus its coverage on immigration? Or, more generically, do the media set trends in society or simply respond to trends that are already underway and just broaden the knowledge and understanding of them?

The term "agenda-setting" appears to have been originally used in research by Maxwell E. McCombs and Donald L. Shaw, which a communication journal published in 1972. In the study, McCombs and Shaw interviewed 100 undecided voters in Chapel Hill, North Carolina, and asked them what issues concerned them the most in the upcoming presidential election of 1968. After determining the five issues the voters considered most vital, the researchers analyzed the print and broadcast media serving Chapel Hill for the content of their stories. They found an almost perfect correlation between the types of stories that were covered most often and the voters' concern for the same issues.[3]

The study done by McCombs and Shaw into agenda-setting was not the first, and it was definitely not to be the last. Each year, several studies are conducted within the various disciplines of agenda-setting research. These disciplines range from the fields of communication, journalism, political science, sociology, and history. Usually, the studies appear to confirm that agenda-setting does occur, and that media focus on stories is the most important factor involved in shaping public opinion about the relative importance of the issues covered. But the studies don't say the media is the *only* influence on those agendas, just the most prevalent and often the most significant influence. Some studies have shown that the number of times the news media repeat a story will affect viewers' or readers' perception of the story's importance, no matter what is actually said about the topic.

Much research into agenda-setting is ongoing today. One prolific researcher into the topic of the role the media play in political agenda-setting is Shanto Iyengar, a professor of political science and communication at UCLA. He has conducted numerous research studies concerning agenda-setting, and he is the author of several books dealing with the effects of television on American politics, including *News That Matters* and *Going Negative: How Political Advertisements Shrink and Polarize the Electorate* (with Stephen Ansolabehere).

AGENDAS AND YOUTH VOTING

The subject of how agenda-setting might influence voter turnout, especially among younger voters, was examined in a recent study by Spiro Kiousis of the University of Florida. This study examined the role of agenda-setting in impacting voter turnout using panel data of adolescents in the states of Arizona, Colorado, and Florida from 2002 and 2004. The researcher developed a model investigating the different influences of interactive civics instruction, media attention, and discussion on the following sequence of outcomes: perceived salience, opinion strength, political ideology, and voter turnout. The findings of the study indicate that agenda-setting provides a critical process in socializing young people to politics, and helps form a young person's political ideologies and assumptions which, in turn, can lead to heavier involvement in the voting process.

Kiousis notes:

> For more than four decades, agenda-setting research has demonstrated that the relative prominence of issues presented in news media is a key predictor of their perceived salience in public opinion...The application of agenda-setting to

political socialization offers an ideal framework to extend research...because civic
development is focused in micro-environmental spheres such as families, classrooms,
and peer groups where youth are most likely to talk about politics and news,
circulate opinions, and develop issue awareness.[4]

This study amplifies previous agenda-setting work and takes it into the arena
of political socialization. It indicates the affective, cognitive, and behavioral
results of adolescents participating in interactive civic education. As Kiousis
explains, peer-oriented discussion in school motivates conversations with
parents at home. Then the discussion between students and parents increases
the value of paying attention to news stories and media commentaries about
politics over time. Attention to the news then engenders issue salience as the
youths begin to acquire a sense of issue importance in the political arena.
Finally, the views of these youths of the relative importance of issues was joined
by more powerful feelings about the American actions in Iraq, and that lends
support to the idea that affective outcomes are part of the agenda-setting
process.[5]

Why is it that some topics generate a lot of public attention, then fade from
view, and later show up again on the public's or government's agenda? How does
the process of agenda-setting actually work? What do academic research and
public mobilization contribute to the agenda-setting process? And what really
causes a social change in attitude from feeling sorry for someone to taking responsibility for action? What, in other words, turns a social issue into a problem that
cries out for action?

As Newton Minnow and Jay Winsten pointed out in 1993, timing is critically
important in deciding when to tackle an issue.

Important issues that arise on the social agenda, such as gun proliferation, drug
abuse, AIDS, and drunk driving, have a natural life history with fairly discrete
stages that may extend over years and even decades. Gun-related violence is
now entering an exponential growth phase. Which responses, including those
involving the mass media, will be most effective in countering this epidemic?
These questions are important not only intellectually but also operationally
for individuals and institutions seeking to influence media, public, and policy
agendas.[6]

It was to discuss these issues that the Annenberg Washington Program and the
Harvard Center for Health Communication organized a national invitational
conference in October 1993 to analyze how many variables impact the
content of the public agenda and the changing of social norms. Conference
participants also looked at how mass communication might be used to maximize
health through its influence on the public agenda, on social norms, and on
individual behavior. The sessions brought together leading scholars, activists,
public opinion analysts, government officials, and business and foundation
leaders, and focused specifically on the prevention of gun-related violence.

In her reflection on the 1993 Annenberg Washington program, Margaret Gerteis took a brief journey through journalistic history to show how the mass media can influence changes in society. Specifically, she returned to January 1903, when S. S. McClure, founder and editor of the popular mass-circulation magazine *McClure's*, drew his readers' attention to the "coincidental" appearance of three articles in that month's issue—one by the famed muckraker Lincoln Steffens on corruption and machine politics in Minneapolis, the second by Ida Tarbell in her continuing history of Standard Oil, and the third a piece by Ray Stannard Baker critical of organized labor's attempts to keep non-union men from working. These were not the first investigative pieces exposing what McClure described as a "contempt for law" in American institutions.

But Gerteis notes that what McClure had discovered was the salience of these issues to his readers; what he glimpsed was the influence that periodicals like this could have on the public's social consciousness. "Capitalists, workingmen, politicians, citizens—all breaking the law, or letting it be broken," he editorialized. "Who is left to uphold it? There is no one left; none but all of us."[7] What followed was a uniquely twentieth century phenomenon: a public crusade, fueled by the popular press, producing, within a decade, sweeping reforms of municipal government and state and federal civil service, electoral reform, pure food and drug regulation, antitrust legislation, and myriad other "progressive" social reforms. With no specific agenda of its own, McClure's nonetheless launched a new era in mass communication and social agenda-setting.

Telescoping ahead in time, Gerteis analyzed another story that effected social change. It came nearly 80 years later, in December 1981, as an editorial in the *New England Journal of Medicine* directed readers' attention to another coincidence—independent reports from the field about the appearance of rare opportunistic illnesses in young homosexual men. Gerteis wondered, what have we learned since McClure's day about how the media shape the social agenda, for good or ill, or influence the public's capacity to take effective action? In the history of the AIDS crisis, did the popular media contribute to unconscionable inaction in the early days by relegating the story to the margins of social deviance? Or did they ultimately help mobilize public opinion around an extraordinarily difficult social issue? Or did they do both? What do we know now about harnessing the power of mass communication to influence public health attitudes or change behavior?

Among those scholars looking for—and not finding much—evidence to support the assumption that objective conditions mold public opinions is Harvard Sociology Professor Nathan Glazer. The issues that might legitimately claim our attention are virtually limitless, yet we are unable to focus on more than a handful at once—between five and seven, to be exact, according to the agenda-setting research of Professor McCombs. The issues may be real enough, but there is no simple means of establishing priorities among these issues just on the basis of the "facts." Further, most of us are not experienced with the social issues that compete for our attention, McCombs asserts. We rely on secondhand information to tell us what is important. Glazer believes that "facts" in the minds of readers or viewers become shaped by the rhetoric and drama of the presenting media, and that this is quite different from an objective reality itself. Shaping the facts to make them more compelling— "creative epidemiology," as Michael Pertschuk, co-director of the Advocacy Institute, terms it—is a practice well-known to advocates for particular social causes.[8]

Of course, one of McComb's key questions was this: If the media shape the public agenda, what shapes the media's agenda? McCombs believes that only about three of ten stories in the mass media "thrust" themselves onto the agenda because of their objective importance to the public. Natural disasters or other public catastrophes, for example, fall into this category. The rest are there because they fit the conventions of journalism: they fill the need for drama, controversy, or human interest; they come from established and "reliable" sources; or they have been deemed worthy of coverage by the *New York Times* or *Washington Post*. But McCombs also believes that the conventions of journalism—the choice of experts, the search for drama, "balance," or controversy—mold the way an issue is framed in the public mind. The mass media tell us not only what to think about, McCombs observes, but also how to think about it.[9]

One story that many scholars point to as an example of how influential the media can be in shaping public opinion was the developing story of the discovery of AIDS in the 1980s. Professor Everett M. Rogers focuses on that continuing story in his analysis of media coverage, polling data, and federal funding statistics. For almost two years after the *New England Journal of Medicine* identified the association between the disease and homosexual men, the major news media, as well as the federal funding agencies and the public in general, virtually ignored AIDS. When researchers discovered the human immunodeficiency virus in 1983, some media made note of the scientific aspects of the disease and its transmission. However, it was not until a Hollywood movie star and a young schoolboy succumbed to the disease—two individuals with whom the white, middle-class, heterosexual public could identify—that the media and the public perceived AIDS as a genuine concern for public health. "The media discovered AIDS not because of statistical measures of its world importance," Rogers asserts, "but because two famous people—Rock Hudson and Ryan White—got it and gave the story a human touch."[10]

PUBLIC OPINION

What is the process that takes place for public opinion to become transformed into public judgment and action? Daniel Yankelovich, chairman of DYG Inc. and WSY Consulting Group, Inc., has noted that the concept of "public opinion" brings forth two polarized images, depending on the situation. One is the notion of a wild beast that must be controlled or kept calm. The other lends a metaphysical, almost deified, status to public opinion. Actually, however, both images may be correct: "Sometimes public opinion on a particular issue seems mindless and thoughtless and irresponsible; sometimes, on the same issue at a later point in time, public opinion seems almost uncannily right," Yankelovich says. What happens, he theorizes, is that "a quite orderly process of evolution occurs on some issues, whereby the incoherent, beastly roar evolves gradually into a coherent public voice—a genuine vox populi."[11]

Yankelovich calls "public judgment" the final, unified public voice as evolved from the "raw" opinion. Transitioning toward public judgment is a convoluted process of sifting through and understanding conflicting emotions, values, and interests that surround a given topic. He says it is unrealistic to expect wisdom, but public judgment suggests a deeper resolution than does the more common notion of a "well-informed" citizenry that reporters appear to evision.

Yankelovich identifies seven gates in the journey from raw opinion to public judgment:[12]

1. Awareness
2. A sense of urgency or a demand for action
3. A search for solutions
4. Reaction and resistance
5. Wrestling with alternative choices
6. Intellectual assent, or resolution at the cognitive level
7. Full resolution—moral, emotional, and intellectual

Yankelovich believes the media can do an excellent job at the start of the process, by putting issues on the public's radar screen and generating a sense of urgency over them. But then the media often move on to the next issue, offering up little to the arduous process of working the problems through. Traditional reporters represent positions as adversarial—positions on issues like abortion or gun control, for example, that rarely correspond to the real views of most people, the public opinion expert notes. But this can actually slow the progress, contributing to the traffic jam that so often sets in when the public tries to understand and deal with these issues. On the other hand, if journalists, especially reporters for the major news media, would perceive their job to instead analyze the conflicting values swirling around an issue, then journalists could become a major contributor in jump-starting the process of public discussion over an issue.

How, then do we focus public attention on more mainstream strategies that would probably garner more support? Yankelovich believes that the mass media have the opportunity to serve as a public forum that can speed up the evolution of public judgment on this issue—a process that literally took decades, in the cases of smoking and drunk driving.

REDEFINING A NATION?

In 2006, a doctoral student at the University of Memphis finished an insightful dissertation on the impact the mainstream media can have on American public perceptions of an entire country, and how that perception can influence political framing of the country. Abdulrahman Abdulla Al-Zuhayyan investigated the construction of Saudi Arabia's social reality before and after Setpember 11, 2001, by American television news organizations ABC, NBC, CBS, and Fox. He also analyzed U.S. government officials' news framing of international news stories such as the 9/11 disaster. Al-Zuhayyan found the *media congruency construction frame* was supported by his research. This frame categorizes the *intensity of symbols* used by the media, and relates them to a *type of political relationship* (normal, dispute, conflict, or war) between the U.S. and a foreign country, which ultimately identified the U.S. relationship with Saudi Arabia as *in conflict*.[13]

In other words, the ways in which Saudi Arabia was depicted by the media led to a very tense relationship between the United States and Saudi Arabia. The study revealed three findings: (a) similarities among U.S. mainstream news organizations in constructing news stories about Saudi Arabia in a conflictive outlook; (b) similarities in covering the variables of this stories; and (c) a relationship between the U.S. government and those news organizations. The study concluded that the U.S. mainstream news organizations constructed Saudi Arabia in ways consistent with U.S. political, economic, and cultural ideologies, as well as U.S. interests and national security lines promoted by U.S. government officials. These news organizations constructed a *conflictive social reality* of Saudi Arabia to pressure Saudi Arabia in complying with the fulfillment of U.S. interests regarding the war on international terrorism.[14]

Al-Zuhayyan notes in his study that, in the days following the 9/11 attacks, the mainstream U.S. media (which he defines as the media that address the audiences who constitute the prevailing thoughts and influence in U.S. society) reported that the majority of the perpetrators of these heinous attacks were Saudi Arabians. Consequently, he explains, Saudi Arabia as a government, people, and culture was associated with the attacks by the mainstream U.S. media and discourse which grew out of that media coverage. The researcher notes that heated TV debates of "Why they hate us" were seen by millions of Americans. The most often quoted media answer was that a radical Islamic ideology called "Wahhabism," which preaches intolerance against nonbelievers of its tenets and hatred of the West (particularly the United States), influenced those terrorists. Moreover, Saudi Arabia was said to embrace this ideology as its official sect of Islam. Observers claimed the country promotes it through its educational system and mosques, and exported it to the Islamic World by building schools (Maddrassa) that teach the ideology. Additionally, media observers said Saudi Arabian individuals, charities, and banks were said to finance terrorist activities. Al-Zuhayyan observes:

Consequently, Saudi Arabia was viewed as creating an atmosphere conducive to terrorist organizations to recruit susceptible and vulnerable Muslims, especially Saudis, to commit terrorist attacks on the United States. In addition, the U.S. mainstream media pointed out that Saudi Arabia restricts these ideologues the freedom of expression at home but encourages them to vent their anger at the United States. The solution that was offered to the problem of Islamic terrorism was the promotion of democratic principles in the Middle East—specifically, in Saudi Arabia—with the road of expanding democracy first going through Iraq. Working from those accusations, U.S. mainstream television news organizations demanded that the U.S. government look at Saudi Arabia as a national security issue and that Saudi Arabia must comply with President George W. Bush's doctrine for combating international terrorism.[15]

The study asserts that most Americans develop their knowledge about foreign countries by watching television. Although Americans perceived Saudi Arabia in a slightly negative light before the events of September 11, 2001, the U.S. mainstream media exacerbated those negative perceptions via their coverage of Saudi Arabia after September 11, 2001. Therefore, the media constructed a unique social reality in the minds of the American public and its government concerning Saudi Arabia.

The cyclical nature of media/government influence can be seen by looking at President Bush's speech on September 20, 2001, declaring a doctrine for combating international terrorism. Al-Zuhayyan's study states this speech "initiated the news frames of international stories in the U.S. mainstream media."[16] These media identified Saudi Arabia as the source of international terrorism. Other researchers have noted that the framing processes that aim for consensus mobilization and action mobilization have four basic functions: (a) identifying the problem and attributing responsibility (in this case, international terrorism/Islamic terrorism, with Saudi Arabia being responsible for it); (b) identifying the cause of the problem (Wahhabism); (c) prescribing a remedy for the problem (democracy); and (d) employing symbols that convey a particular judgment (a negative perception of Saudi Arabia).[17]

HURRICANE KATRINA

In a 2006 study, researcher Fred Vultee at the University of Missouri performed a content analysis of national news coverage of Hurricane Katrina's impact and aftermath. In it he examined how blame was apportioned between local and national actors, and what the effects are when stories are told from personal or institutional perspectives, which areas of impact are highlighted, and—perhaps most significantly—whether a *media agenda* of long-term hazard mitigation emerges.[18] The study's findings revealed a significant negative change in depictions of the federal government's role and a corresponding decline in public approval of President Bush's handling of the hurricane and its aftermath.

The study was also interesting in that it looked at news coverage of Katrina and its aftermath, along with data from public opinion polls, to determine which aspects of a disaster like Katrina get the lion's share of news coverage. From that, it examined which aspects are then transitioned to the public's agenda. The study emphasized two issues:

1. Mitigation. The Federal Emergency Management Agency (FEMA) defines this concept as "any sustained action taken to reduce or eliminate long-term risk to life and property from a hazard event." As Vultee notes, mitigation deals less with helping disaster victims than with the measures taken to reduce the possibility of a particular kind of hazard or minimize its impact on people or property.
2. Attribution. This is the degree to which blame, credit, and/or responsibility are apportioned among the various actors in the event.

Vultee explains that mitigation traditionally gets less news coverage than other aspects of a disaster such as the "sensation of the moment" or the return of a semblance of order out of the chaos. The researcher continues:

> Related concerns grow out of the study of framing. Does the portrayal of events "as though they were the result of the president's actions" (Iyengar and Kinder, 1987, p. 82) lead audiences to apportion credit and blame inappropriately among the actors involved? Similarly, does the use of frames that emphasize "personalized case histories" (Iyengar and Simon, 1987, p. 36), known as episodic or vivid frames, affect the attribution of responsibility differently from the thematic or pallid frames that emphasize structural issues, trends and other abstract matters? Indeed, if vulnerability is bounded by class rather than by adverse reactions in some unnamed system, the victim frame in Hurricane Katrina has a ring of social justice to it as well. But if attention to individual plights draws news resources away from attention to potential systemic flaws, such justice would be limited in its scope.[19]

Specifically, Vultee's study, based on a content analysis of news stories in USA Today, found that "if a mitigation frame emerges as an important part of disaster coverage, it does so late, and its significance is questionable."[20] The researcher further notes, "Personal-frame articles (stories focusing on individual people) are most common in the impact, accounting for just over a third of the total, and recovery, again accounting for about a third of the total, phases." The personal-frame articles were seen most during the second and third weeks after impact. The findings also note that, "In the week after the storm struck, the impact most frequently mentioned (38.8 percent) is on the national economy; the impact on individuals or on general health and safety concerns comprised just over a third of the stories."[21] Finally, in terms of how effective the leaders are in carrying out their responsibilities after the storm, here is what the study found: In the week after the storm's impact, the enthusiasm expressed by evacuees for federal assistance ran alongside their anger over local government. But, within a matter of weeks, coverage of the federal role became significantly less favorable. In fact, all of the articles from November portrayed the federal government negatively. Additionally, President Bush's handling of Katrina was drawing negative reviews at the same time. In the week following the storm, one survey found that Bush had a 54 percent approval rating for his performance, against 12 percent who disapproved. But the following week his approval rating was down to 35 percent, while 42 percent disapproved. It was during these weeks that the White House decided to promote more coverage of the president going to New Orleans and of the positive things he was doing for the victims of Katrina.

SPECIFYING TERMINOLOGY

Of course it does little good to say the media set the agenda when both the terms "media" and "agenda" can refer to many different things. To lump all media influence together and lay it at the doorstep of "the media" is to say that—as a group and individually—newspapers, magazines, radio, the Internet, cable television and broadcast television all have equal, or at least similar effects on the government's agenda. Clearly that is not the case. The media used by the greatest percentage of a senator's or congressman's constituents have the greatest power. Therefore, the most effective agenda-setting studies are those which focus on a specific medium and its impact on the public's agenda.

An odd thing when it comes to media agenda-setting is that we don't always know the origin of that power or influence. Today's media are an impersonal collection of institutions, and the World Wide Web has made them even more so. Editors and journalism professors often counsel their charges to beware of Internet sourcing, because often the original sources of information on various Web sites are unknown. Many years ago, author Edward Jay Epstein wrote a book called *News from Nowhere* in which he discussed the notion that news just seems to automatically originate without personality, bias, or perspective from somewhere within the bowels of the media. In their book, *Media and Society: The Production of Culture in the Mass Media,* authors John Ryan and William Wentworth have this to say about the media's impersonality:

> New technologies have altered one or more of these elements of face-to-face com-
> munication. The written word removes most of everything but the obvious content.
> While the context may be well understood in the particular tie and place of the
> document's creation, it becomes less obvious as it moves outside its own culture
> and time period. For example, Wendy Griswold (1987) has shown how the novels
> of West Indian writer George Lamming have been interpreted differently by literary
> critics from the West Indies, Great Britain, and the United States...One way of
> describing these effects is to say that much of modern communication is impersonal,
> while much communication in traditional society is personal. But it's not quite that
> simple. Technologies such as television and the Internet are capable of mimicking
> elements of face-to-face communication. Television, for example, shows visual

images of human faces that can, especially in advertising and newscasts, seem to speak directly to viewers. Messages are often designed to appeal to familiar situations and strong emotions. Thus, modern societies are awash in communication that appears to be personal but lacks some crucial elements of the personal. From a societal standpoint, one of the most crucial of these missing elements is the ability to judge the accuracy of the message.[22]

So the media have this impersonal quality that masquerades as a personal one, and they also dump an enormous amount of information everyday on a public that must somehow sort through it all, make sense of it, and assimilate it into their daily lives. The day of *real-time reporting* arrived in the 1990s, and information delivery has increased by warp speed since then. Whether on the Internet, iPod, or television, we now have raw information at our fingertips. It is news as it is happening, and thus it is often news devoid of helpful context needed for a clear understanding of it. For journalists, the stakes have only risen for the need of getting the story right, even in the midst of intense media competition where there is a deadline almost every second.

NONTRADITIONAL MEDIA EFFECTS

As is noted elsewhere in this book, the traditional news media have seen their public clout diminished by the fascination Americans are having with more nontraditional media forms. The influence of these newer venues of news and commentary was the subject of a 2004 study by William P. Eveland. This study shows that "nontraditional political communication forms are finally producing consistent positive effects equivalent to traditional media such as television news and newspapers. Moreover there is some evidence that these positive effects may be amplified among the less educated, helping to close the knowledge gap."[23]

By nontraditional political communication forms, Eveland is speaking of non-news programming, quasi-news/talk shows like "Larry King Live," talk radio like the Rush Limbaugh show, or even late-night comedy shows such as "Late Night with David Letterman" or "The Tonight Show with Jay Leno". The study notes that the 2004 presidential election campaign used more of these nontraditional communication forms, and that the influence of these programs was just as strong as their more traditional communication counterparts such as network and local news programming. Eveland notes that the findings also imply these effects may be even stronger for those viewers with lower educational levels. This, he suggests, may be a good sign when it comes to reducing the size of the knowledge gap between education levels of American society.[24]

The findings are based on data from three different studies performed during 2004. These studies were a Media Consumption Study done by the Pew Center (which included the biggest number of nontraditional media variables of all three studies), an American National Election Study, and a Battleground State

Study conducted by Strategic Research Group (in which researchers conducted telephone interviews for three weeks following the 2004 presidential election).

In conclusion, Eveland notes, "With the exception of cable news, each form of both traditional and nontraditional media use had a positive, unique, and statistically significant relationship with political knowledge."[25] One reason cable news may not show higher in increasing political knowledge is that younger viewers tend not to watch cable news, at least not in the numbers older viewers do.

The obvious impact of findings such as the Eveland study is that national political candidates are making greater use of nontraditional media forms than ever before, and that this will only increase in years to come. Even candidates for state offices are doing this, as happened when Arnold Schwarzenegger, the pending 2003 Republican candidate for governor of California, made an appearance on the Jay Leno show in the campaign season for that special election. As he sat in the chair normally reserved for entertainers (such as himself in his former role), Schwarzenegger laid out the key things he thought Gov. Gray Davis had done wrong for California, and what he thought should be done instead. A short time later he made his announcement for candidacy official. And a few years earlier, of course, Democratic presidential candidate Bill Clinton appeared on the Arsenio Hall Show playing his saxophone.

NEWS FRAMING

Still another societal effect of the media is its ability to either factionalize an audience or bring it together with a sense of shared identity. Stories which focus on polarized debates and which omit discussion of any common ground are likely to produce more polarity among the reading or viewing public. That is one of the problems associated with the traditional newspaper reporting structure known as the *inverted pyramid*. That story structure requires journalists to lead with "the most important" or "the most controversial" parts of the story, and to defer details (often mitigating ones) until later in the story. A key element of the lead is *polarity or conflict*, and journalists often pump up that conflict to its highest legitimate level for optimal reader interest. The stronger the conflict, the stronger the lead, and thus the stronger the story. The strongest stories get the best play in the newspaper, and the thinking behind the inverted pyramid is to give readers a summary of the "important" parts of the story in the first two or three paragraphs, so, if they don't go any further, they will know the story. The problem, of course, is that what this cursory reader gets is the *conflict*, but not the mitigating details and context of it.

A helpful trend in the news industry is the shift that has taken place in many newspapers to the narrative style of reporting. The narrative style, in a way, stands the inverted pyramid on its head, beginning with some of the telling details before moving to the "nut graph" which relates the summary of the story, and tying the opening anecdote to the body of the story. Often these telling details allow us to get to know the key people involved in the story in a more intimate way and to understand and identify with them. This kind of reporting and writing can help greatly in allowing readers to experience a shared identity.

MEDIATED REALITY AT HOME

The news media help frame reality not only on foreign issues, but also on domestic issues. The earlier discussion of Hurricane Katrina is one example of this domestic framing effect, but there are many others. In a series of studies done by *Public Opinion Quarterly*, researchers found media disclosures on a series of domestic issues that were influential in changing the attitudes of government policymakers. The first of these studies, conducted in 1983, concluded that a nationally televised investigative news report on fraud and abuse in the federally funded home health care program had significant effects on the agenda of both the public and policymakers. Actual policy changes also resulted, albeit more from direct pressure for change by the journalists themselves.

A second study the group did in 1985 looked at the impact of a *Chicago Sun-Times* investigative series revealing government irregularities in the way city rape cases were reported and handled. In response to the series, legislators held hearings, and Chicago city officials looked inward to see how they could clean up these improprieties. An interesting effect of the series was that many more and longer stories about rape began appearing in the pages of the Sun-Times. It seems that, not only did the series increase the salience of rape cases for city and state officials, it did the same for editors at the Sun-Times.

The third investigative report was a five-part local television series entitled "Beating Justice," about brutality by some Chicago police officers. The reporting had a strong effect on viewer attitudes about police brutality, and brought about some major revisions within the Chicago Police Department.

The fourth study analyzed the public opinion and policymaking impact of a Chicago television series about the toxic waste disposal habits of the University of Chicago. One of the main targets of the series was the Chicago Fire Department and its regulatory safety practices regarding hazardous waste disposal. Like the other series, policymaking changes resulted in the fire department making changes, although—like the home health care series—some of these changes resulted from outright journalistic lobbying through city officials.

Summing up the results of the four studies, the researchers noted that three of the four investigative reports caused general public impact, two caused impact among the city's elite, and all four resulted in some type of policymaking response and/or change. It is significant that one investigative series that did not result in either general public or elite impact was done by a newspaper, while the three others were television series. That probably underscores the fact that television has become such a prominent influence with the public and, therefore, with the government policymakers.

In conclusion, the researchers noted:

> For public attitudes to change, two factors seem to be important—the nature of the media portrayal and the frequency of attention by the media to the issue in the past. When the media portray an issue in an unambiguous way with dramatic, convincing and clear evidence, public attitudes are more likely to change. In sum, the actual importance or seriousness of a problem may be less significant for influencing public attitudes than its "mediated reality." The second factor...is the nature of the issue that the media are addressing. Certain issues receive fairly consistent treatment by journalists. Investigative stories about recurring issues have lower impact potential. We would suggest that news media investigative reports with the maximum ability to produce attitude change are those that involve unambiguous presentations of nonrecurring issues.[26]

CHAPTER 6

Decoding the News: A Primer in Media Literacy

What are readers or viewers to make of the torrent of media stories cascading upon them, day in and day out? How are they supposed to decide which are told objectively, which subjective treatments might offer the most truthful understanding of the issue, event, or person, and which reporters are trustworthy and deserve the mantle of credibility? Other questions also confront the news consumer and are often the subject of debate and critiques about the media. These questions include the following: Do television executives care mostly about ratings instead of informing us accurately on issues and events important to us? Is it right for some journalists to show their emotions or outrage over tragedies they witness? Is it right for them to show anger to respected government officials if they feel the social problems are not being corrected? Am I witnessing an attempt by unseen interests to manipulate or persuade me to a point of view? After all, aren't the media mostly made up of liberals? Why should I trust these liberal journalists to represent conservative viewpoints accurately? Conversely, aren't the media too tied to mainstream institutions in society, and therefore only interested in perpetuating the status quo?

These and other questions and issues confront the reader or viewer as they ponder the scope and kind of coverage they receive over the airways or cable, through their newspapers or magazines, over radio, or through the Internet. This chapter is an attempt to offer ways of answering some of these questions and, in the process, to provide a degree of media literacy to those who feel in need of it to better understand the news and the news media.

THE JOURNALIST AS A CLUE

To begin our journey through the maze of journalism, it might be helpful to stop first and take a look at the journalist. In communication theory parlance, the journalist is the gatekeeper: that individual who opens or closes the gate to the event, issue, or person he or she chooses to call news. Knowing something about the gatekeepers in America should help news consumers understand better the stories they produce. As we saw in Chapter 5, news stories are not the reality themselves, only representations of reality. So, in large measure, news consumers are dependent upon a person they do not know—or often do not know about—to bring them a focused and accurate picture of reality. So who is this individual, and is the conventional wisdom many hold of him or her being a fire-breathing liberal accurate itself? During the late twentieth century, some serious attempts were made at defining the American journalist and, as a matter of fact, *The American Journalist* was the title of a book by a group of researchers at the University of Indiana in 1971. This comprehensive study of American journalists was updated three other times, in 1982, 1992, and 2002 under a grant from the John S. and James L. Knight Foundation. The study is based on extended telephone interviews with 1,149 full-time journalists (both print and broadcast) in the summer and fall of 2002. Following are some of the key findings from the 2002 edition of this survey:[1]

- Only about 37 percent of full-time journalists said they were Democrats, and that figure is 7 percent fewer than the 1992 survey. This moves journalists closer to the overall percentage of Americans who say they are Democrats. Some media critics who continue to label most journalists as liberals might be surprised at this finding.

- Almost 19 percent of full-time journalists said they were Republicans, about a 2 percent jump from the 1992 survey. Some 31 percent of all Americans say they are Republicans.

- About one-third of all journalists said they were Independents, almost identical to the figure for all U.S. adults.

- Journalistic values persist in the face of profit pressures their news organizations are facing from management and owners. This put them at odds with their perception of what the owners value most. For example, most journalists felt that maintaining as large an audience as possible is the owners' primary motive, while earning high profits ranked second, and producing quality journalism was third. To most journalists, producing quality journalism is the highest priority. Almost two-thirds of journalists believed that, despite profit pressure on the newsrooms, that the quality of journalism was still rising at their news operation.

- American journalists rank their journalistic training as the strongest influence on their decisions regarding what constitutes news. In fact, training seems to be a value most journalists respect, as some two-thirds said they had received additional training since becoming a journalist.

- More than 70 percent of journalists say the "watchdog" role of journalists is the most important role they have, especially when it comes to investigating government.
- More journalists believe it is more important to get the story right than getting it first.
- Undercover reporting continues to be a controversial practice in American journalists, with just over half of the responding journalists supporting this kind of deceptive reporting tactic.
- About the same percentage of journalists—just over 50 percent—support the practice of badgering unwilling informants to get a story.
- Just over three-fourths of all journalists supported using confidential business or government documents without authorization.
- Overall, about one-third of all full-time journalists are women—the same percentage as 1982—but the number of women in the younger ranks are increasing dramatically. Among journalists with fewer than five years of experience, women outnumber men, 54–46 percent.
- The percentage of full-time journalists of color working for mainstream media is increasing, albeit slightly. Among all journalists with less than five years experience, about 17 percent are people of color. Television employs the highest percentage of journalists of color. Still, with about 30 percent of the American population comprised of people of color, the diversity in the newsroom still lags the national percentage.

Another of the serious attempts at defining a journalist was done by sociologist Herbert J. Gans, and the book that resulted from his content analysis of several of the country's "elite" media was called simply *Deciding What's News*. As was explained in Chapter 5, one of the things the Gans study did was to judge which—if any—lasting or "enduring" values were contained in a cross-section of print and broadcast stories from some of the best media outlets in the United States in the early 1980s. What he found was a list of eight enduring values surfacing from these stories and, by way of quick review, they are: ethnocentrism, altruistic democracy, leadership, order, moderatism, responsible capitalism, small-town pastoralism, and rugged individualism.[2] Building from that base, Gans asked if these values—since they appeared to be embedded in a variety of news stories—might not be reflective of the values journalists themselves hold? It would make sense, since these are the values journalists write about either when someone upholds them or when someone or something threatens them. Gans went further in asking whether these could really be called "liberal" values, which many media critics believe are the kind that journalists hold. His conclusion: these are mainstream American values and reflect more of a reformist attitude than a liberal set. In fact, some of those values could be construed as downright conservative in nature.

Other attempts have been made to study the nature of journalists, and they have taken the form of additional studies in scholarly journals such as *Journalism & Mass Communication Quarterly* and the*Newspaper Research Journal*.

Another way of looking at journalists is to ask what propels individuals into this controversial, and relatively low-paying, profession in the first place. Some feel that a prime motivator for many would-be journalists is a sense of outrage at society and a driving ambition to attack the existing power structure in America, especially if it is a conservative power structure. Alas, like those who enter any profession, the reasons are many and varied for journalistic hopefuls. In almost four decades as either a journalist or journalism professor, I have seen almost every conceivable reason motivating individuals to become journalists. Some have simply wanted to change the world, to make it a better place to live. Others have developed a love of writing and want a career where they can write everyday. Still others have a desire to be on the inside, to be "in the know." They are the ones who want to be first to tell others what they have just learned, to break the story first. Others are drawn to the independence of the job. They have a sense that journalists get to work on their own projects, and often at their own pace. Still others just love the creative process of starting with a blank laptop screen and finishing with a publishable story. And then others are drawn to the dynamic route of a journalist where no two days are seldom the same.

One clue to what motivates journalists can be found in a survey done that became the cornerstone of a doctoral thesis at the University of Missouri School of Journalism on newsroom management. In part, that survey asked reporters what they liked best about their jobs, and here is how they responded:[3]

- Making a difference in the world; exposing the wrongdoing and corruption.
- Being on the inside of issues; getting to know important people.
- The whole creative process of reporting and writing.
- Learning new things everyday about people and how the world operates.
- Producing work on deadline, and then starting all over the next day.
- The variety that exists in the job of gathering the news and writing it.

Still another clue to what journalists are like comes from the way their jobs dictate, to some degree anyway, how they conduct their personal lives. Many journalists have an inborn apprehension about joining groups or causes for fear that, one day, they may have to report on that group or cause. They don't want to appear biased (and certainly don't want to actually be biased) in covering the story, so they often choose not to join any groups at all. One of the ethical issues often discussed among journalists and written about in journalism textbooks is this very issue of the journalist as a joiner. It is often seen as stepping over the line for a journalist to join a protest or demonstration, or to join in an election campaign, or to serve as a spokesman or advocate for any particular cause. Others believe journalists should be able to exercise the right all Americans have to join whatever groups or causes, or to campaign for whoever they like. After all, these defenders say, these are Constitutional rights granted to everyone, and journalists have a right to contribute as good citizens like everyone else.

Nevertheless, for many journalists who have been caught in a bind by supporting one cause over another, this is a tricky path to walk. Once, as an editor in Texas, I decided to join in and support the local humane society. This is certainly an innocent enough cause, I reasoned. How could any harm come from supporting it? Then one day two groups came before the City Council seeking funding, and there was only enough money for one of them. And one of the groups was the local humane society. The issue became the source of much debate at the council meeting, and my paper covered it. The humane society prevailed and received the city's grant, and I was tagged by some in town as the reason for it. The thinking was that somehow the City Council knew I was a staunch supporter of the humane society, and the fact I was editor of the local paper influenced them to vote as they did. I exercised no influence at all and stayed out of the issue entirely, but the appearance remained the same to some in town: the editor had swayed the council vote.

Yet another clue to how some journalists operate is found—sadly—in some high-profile cases of journalists who have decided to put loyalty to their own career over loyalty to the truth. I am speaking here of the well-known cases of journalists like Jayson Blair, formerly of the *New York Times*; Stephen Glass, formerly of *The New Republic*; and—further in the past—of Janet Cooke, formerly of the *Washington Post*. Each of these journalists made decisions to engage in deceptive practices that went far beyond the occasional embellishment of a quote or the hyping of a lead. In the case of Jayson Blair, the *New York Times* discovered invention of sources and the quotes and attributions that came along with them; in the case of Stephen Glass, *The New Republic* found more than two dozen of his stories were about events that never happened or people who never lived. This reporter's practices were so egregious that a movie was made depicting his exploits, aptly titled *Shattered Glass*. The young reporter, who was drawing a six-figure salary writing for *The New Republic*, *George*, and *Rolling Stone* magazines, was brought down when a competitive publication, *Forbes Digital*, probed a story Glass did called "Hack Heaven" and discovered it was total fiction. The infamous case involving Janet Cooke concerned a story she did on an alleged eight-year-old heroin addict. Dubbed "Jimmy's World," the story provided a heart-wrenching account of how a young unnamed boy was introduced to heroin by his mother's boyfriend and became addicted. The story created outrage in Washington, D.C., as police scrambled to find the boy, unaided by Cooke, who refused to name him in the interest of confidentiality. The story was so good it ultimately won journalism's highest honor: the Pulitzer Prize. When *Washington Post* editors (including then metro editor Bob Woodward) discovered the story was a hoax, the paper issued a painful national apology and returned the Pulitzer the story had won.

Exploits such as the ones pulled by these reporters serve only to give journalists and their stories a black eye. The fact that they are so well-written and so engaging exacerbates the problem, causing future readers to wonder, "If those stories were hoaxes and yet were so well-written, how do I know the story I'm reading now is not a hoax, too?"

Much responsibility is laid at the foot of fact-checkers, which top magazines have on staff. Newspapers do not employ fact-checkers per se, but the various line editors are supposed to include that in their responsibilities. However, given their other duties and the flood of news and feature stories which a daily publication produces, fact-checking at newspapers is a tougher proposition than at magazines which come out weekly or monthly. Still, as the Stephen Glass example shows, even the best magazines are vulnerable to mistakes. Glass's editor, Chuck Lane, was asked by 60 Minutes reporter Steve Kroft why the magazine's fact-checkers didn't catch Glass' mistakes. He responded that the magazine was up against someone who had been a fact-checker himself, knew how to subvert the system, and who was intentional in his efforts to deceive the magazine and its readers. Glass neutralized any questions from fact-checkers or Lane by producing fake notes, writing about people who never existed so they never called to complain, and even produced fake Web sites for fake companies.

News consumers should know that reporters like these are anomalies in the journalism profession. That is why they and their actions become news stories and even movies: because they are so far from the norm, so unique. And, as an earlier chapter noted, uniqueness makes news, especially when it threatens the value of moderatism. News consumers should also know that, while all publications and news programs make mistakes, the most renown of this media (as typified by New York Times, Associated Press, Washington Post, Boston Globe, Los Angeles Times, The New Republic, CBS, CNN, etc.) have achieved their status largely because of the credibility they have earned over the decades. A textbook case of how closely many editors guard their newsroom credibility is seen in the classic film, All the President's Men. The film, which came from the book of the same title, depicts the Watergate cover-up by the Nixon Administration and its exposure by the Washington Post. Executive Editor Ben Bradlee, along with reporters Bob Woodward and Carl Bernstein, were tireless in their efforts to insure accuracy and to refrain from rushing into print with stories that were not double-checked, and in many cases, triple-checked.

Still another aid to deciphering the news presentations of the day comes from the various perspectives or orientations that journalists take into their craft. The way a journalist approaches a story has a definite effect on the kind of story that is produced. Hence, these different orientations can provide an important clue into news stories. Among the various perspectives which journalist take to their craft are what I call the following: the traditional, the investigative, the participative, the literary, the economic, the pseudo, the village, and the virtual. You can add to these a straight-out opinion perspective that has come to define some journalists, especially on cable television, and what I call a passionate perspective, which is also appearing more and more on TV and in print. I have chronicled some of these perspectives in detail in other books, but I'll take a fresh look at them here and add on the two not discussed in other projects:

The Traditional Perspective. When I think of this orientation, I think of the old Joe Friday detective character on the TV series, *Dragnet*. One of the favorite lines of this no-nonsense detective was, "Just the facts, ma'am." That is very much the theme of the traditional journalist who is interested in only the facts of a story and believes strongly they can be arranged in a way to form an objective story. The story produced follows the inverted pyramid format (explained below), which does not allow for the literary flourishes found in other writing styles. The traditionalist also believes in using the most neutral of verbiage (what Hayakawa would call "report language"). Most traditionalists stop at the level of accurate facts, and do not necessarily believe in stringing them together to form a "larger truth."

The Investigative Perspective. The investigative journalist takes the traditionalist approach one step further into trying to open up stories that are difficult because someone else is usually sitting on the lid. These are not the daily news stories of most reporters, but require a great deal of time and strategizing to circumvent the forces trying to obfuscate or, in some cases, lie about what is actually going on. The key dilemma faced by investigative journalists is often the question of means-over-ends and how far a journalist should go to get the truth. The classic investigative story—or series of stories—was Watergate, and *Washington Post* reporters Bob Woodward and Carl Bernstein often came up against closed doors (figuratively and literally) in trying to uncover this story of culpability in a massive cover-up operation. In their book, *All the President's Men*, and the subsequent film, the two journalists discuss some of the questions they had at the time about their methods.

The Participative Perspective. In many ways, this method is at the opposite end of the spectrum from the traditionalist. While the traditionalist values detachment from a story, the participative journalist believes that a reporter should become involved in the story to sample first-hand what the characters in the story are going through. You could use the old "smell of the greasepaint, roar of the crowd" metaphor to form the justification for this perspective. Historically, this perspective was practiced by writers such as the late George Plimpton, who, in writing the story "Paper Tiger," assumed the role of an unknown college quarterback trying to make the Detroit Tigers team in training camp. Much more recently, some would call the embedded reporters in Iraq participative reporters. Certainly they put themselves on the front lines with the troops they cover and expose themselves to danger. Some have died in that role, and others like ABC's Bob Woodruff have suffered severe injuries from roadside bombs.

The Literary Perspective. The literary journalist values the telling of the story almost as much as the facts themselves. In some cases, he or she values it even more. Author Tom Wolfe would sometimes go beyond what actually happened or what actually was said to what would have probably happened or probably have been said, given the nature of the people in the story. The literary journalist usually eschews the traditionalist's inverted pyramid format and instead embraces the narrative format which novelists use. This writer is looking to tell the story from the beginning, through the rising action to the climax, then to the falling action and final denouement. Writers like Wolfe and Truman Capote (*In Cold Blood*) might have been the first high-profile journalists to bring this perspective into mainstream journalism, but it is practiced by many current writers, including Sebastian Junger, who wrote the best-selling book *The Perfect Storm*. In his foreword to this story about six commercial swordfishermen lost at sea, Junger explains that he has tried to construct a solid piece of journalism that stays true to the facts yet does not "asphyxiate" under a mountain of technical detail. And, to bring that off, he uses the narrative format and blends in other writing techniques that novelists might use in telling this non-fiction story. Junger writes:

> Recreating the last days of six men who disappeared at sea presented some obvious problems for me. On the one hand, I wanted to write a completely factual book that would stand on its own as a piece of journalism. On the other hand, I didn't want the narrative to asphyxiate under a mass of technical detail and conjecture. I toyed with the idea of fictionalizing minor parts of the story—conversations, personal thoughts, day-to-day routeines—to make it more readable, but that risked diminishing the value of whatever facts I was able to determine. In the end I wound up sticking strictly to the facts, but in as wide-ranging a way as possible. If I didn't know exactly what happened about the doomed boat, for example, I would interview people who had been through similar situations and survived. Their experiences, I felt, would provide a fairly good description of what the six men on the Andrea Gail had gone through, and said, and perhaps even felt...In short, I've written as complete an account as possible of something that can never be fully known. It is exactly that unknowable element, however, that has made it an interesting book to write and, I hope, to read.[4]

The Economic Perspective. In the Ron Howard-directed movie *The Paper*, actress Glenn Close plays a hard-driving managing editor of a mythical New York daily, *The Sun*. Although a newswoman at heart, she is given the responsibility for bringing the newspaper in on budget, and her editorial decisions are often based on that premise. This is an example of the economic perspective of journalism: a desire to do a good job telling the news but, most of all, a desire to tell it in a way that will sell, and to know when some stories are too costly to chase. The cost-benefit ratio is assigned to the process of daily journalism, and that ratio is the driving force when push comes to shove over issues about what stories to cover and when to "go with what we've got." This perspective is also the driving force behind the mixing of news and entertainment in television news, and behind the myriad of viewership and readership studies done by the major media. News is therefore defined, largely, as what the viewers and readers say they want. In the print word, Gannett's *USA Today*, which was launched in 1982, is a direct result of market research studies that asked the public nationwide what they want in a newspaper. If that mix includes more color, shorter stories, and more attention to celebrities and fads, then so be it. Not surprisingly, many observers see these qualities as the essence of *USA Today*. The economic perspective is necessitated in many cases by the reality that most media companies are publicly owned and traded on the stock exchange, and management realizes the fiduciary responsibility it has to investors who really care about nothing but return on their investments. The well-respected magazine, *Columbia Journalism Review*, has often looked at this issue of bottom-line journalism. In one article, writer Tim Jones noted:

> [Wall Street analysts] may have as much to say about the long-term future of newspaper journalism as they do about the short-term performance of earnings and stock prices. The clash between meeting investors' financial expectations and protecting journalistic integrity may be approaching a critical juncture...the mind-set of cutting in the interest of "enhancing shareholder value"—pushing up the company earnings—raises questions about the future of a whole range of newspaper operations, from news holes to Sunday magazines, to foreign bureaus.[5]

The Psuedo Perspective. When readers see stories on television or in the newspapers which seem to treat the unreal as the real, they are watching or reading pseudo-news stories. Much entertainment news falls into this category. For example, we all know the events portrayed on *Desperate Housewives* are fictional, but we read stories about it anyway. And there are plenty of stories about this kind of "news." But pseudo-news is found in political coverage, as well, as reporters often flock to staged events and "photo-ops" arranged by White House public relations people, or by a myriad of political consultants for other office-holders and candidates from Washington down to the grass-roots level of politics. Historian Daniel Boorstin, in his classic book, *The Image: a Guide to Pseudo-Events in America*, noted that pseudo-events are often covered as news because that's what the public wants. He explains that the public often wants something bigger, more entertaining, more bizarre than what they saw or read yesterday, and that the news media (largely television) is rushing to provide it for them. And he wrote all this in 1961. It seems even more true today. Boorstin defines the pseudo-event as that which is staged, as opposed to spontaneous; dramatic by design, and which values shadow over substance. In other words, a pseudo-event has little—if any—real significance to the reader or viewer.[6]

The Village Perspective. When a journalist approaches his or her craft as an anthropologist would, a reader could call this the village perspective to the story. The distinguishing feature of this approach is to spend time in the midst of the people you write about; sometimes a long time. It is therefore close to the partici-pative approach, but the reporter only becomes involved to a certain extent, and the story is about others and not the reporter. I call it the village perspective because of a former journalist, Richard Critchfield, who left daily journalism jobs with the *Washington Star* and *Economist* to devote his energies to living in third world villages and describing life there. His thesis was that to really understand what is happening in the world, you have to go to the villages of the world and stay there, sometime for months at a time. It is at this grassroots level, Critchfield believes, that the true story of the world starts emerging. For him, that story is the struggle for much of the world to adapt to Western ways and values. Here is how Critchfield framed it:

> My work, for example, has convinced me that the place to go if you want to under-stand the assassination of Indira Gandhi...is to a Sikh Punjabi village. The same is true if you want to understand the Lebanese Moslem terrorists, the conflict in El Salvador, Africa's food and farming crisis, almost any problem you can name—even America's farming crisis—because village reporting does not work only in the Third World. Go out and live in a village, three weeks, three months, work with the people, share their lives, listen to what they have to say, write is all down and type up your notes. The reality of what you have found will be so plain that the story will practically have written itself. When you look at the world this way it becomes a vast, ongoing revolutionary drama in perpetual movement, in which countless individual actors—the villagers and city slum dwellers alike—are making choices and taking actions to learn, adapt, grow and survive. Some cultures adapt more easily than others.[7]

The Virtual Perspective. This approach bears some resemblance to the pseudo-approach discussed earlier, but it differs in that this reporting is often about events that can have great significance for the reader or viewer. Yet this time it is the reporter or news organization that takes liberties in helping either to recreate—or even stage—the event, or to report on what might have actually happened, had it happened at all. Confused? A couple examples might help. On January 4, 1993, the NBC Nightly News aired a story about a lot of dead fish in Idaho's Clearwater National Forest. The report, and accompanying video of the ill-fated fish, were intended to show the dangers of the timber industry practice of clear-cutting forests; how it contaminates streams and leaves fish dead. The problem, as NBC learned later, is that the dead fish were not from Clearwater and the fish from Clearwater were very much alive. While there is no evidence that this particular event was staged, such was not the case with the embarrassing Dateline NBC episode in which a GM pickup truck exploded on impact with another vehicle. The explosion was meant to show how vulner-able the GM pickup and its uniquely placed gas tank were to side impacts. The problem here, however, was that the GM pickup had been rigged with a charge to explode on cue and on camera. NBC apologized for that incident, and replaced its news division president shortly thereafter.

As writer John Leo notes, in cases like these, the issue is whether the viewer is witnessing simple inaccuracy or outright deception. Here is how Leo saw it in a 1993 essay in *U.S. News & World Report*:

What if it wasn't a lapse? What if it was a preview of what news is destined to become, as images, story line and emotional impact begin to erode the old commitment to literal truth? Richard Reeves, a syndicated columnist with good contacts in the world of TV, explicitly makes this argument. Reeves says the old guard has disappeared from TV news, and the business is now in the hands of a new generation whose members don't think of themselves as reporters or producers, but as filmmakers, with little interest in words and heavy interest in dramatic effect. To Reeves, the GM truck explosions are a watershed event, "the end of the old standards, those old journalism ethics imposed, sometimes quite hypocritically, by print journalists..." CBS News was accused of staging combat scenes in Afghanistan. ABC News "re-enacted" a scene that nobody ever proved was enacted at all—a U.S. diplomat taking a briefcase full of money from Soviet agents. These events put NBC's current problems in perspective.[8]

The Opinion Perspective. A hallmark of most journalistic orientations is that a reporter separates his or her opinion from the facts of the story, and that the story focuses on the latter. Interpretation is allowed in journalism, but the making of value statements and mixing opinion with facts is generally looked upon with disfavor. Not so, however, with some journalists, a few of which have achieved high-profile status on cable news networks like CNN and Fox News. Journalists like Bill O'Reilly, who parades his opinions as facts on his Fox news show "The O'Reilly Factor," and CNN's Lou Dobbs, who anchors the nightly "Lou Dobbs Tonight" hour, have created quite a following of viewers who share their viewpoints. Industry observers refer to this brand of reporting as "opinion journalism," and it has become controversial within the news business. Writing on this perspective in the *New York Times*, reporter Rachel L. Swarns said the following:

> Night after night, Lou Dobbs slides into his anchor chair, turns to the camera and becomes the sober and steady face of CNN. At 60, he has more than three decades of experience, silvering hair and a voice that rumbles with authority. And for most of his program, he looks and feels like a traditional, nothing-but-the-news television host. Then the topic turns to illegal immigration, and the sober newsman starts breathing fire. Mr. Dobbs batters the Bush administration for doing too little to stop millions of migrants from slipping across the border with Mexico. He slams business and advocacy groups for helping illegal aliens thrive here...As his scorching commentaries spill across the nation's television screens, first-time viewers might be forgiven for rubbing their eyes in wonder...But Mr. Dobbs remains unapologetic. He says he has no interest in assuming the conventional role of the anchor who reports the news dispassionately. His mission, he says, is to tell American viewers the truth, no matter how uncomfortable or controversial.[9]

Neither Dobbs nor O'Reilly have pioneered this brand of opinion journalism, as other mainstream journalists have dabbled in it since the Revolutionary days of Samuel Adams, Benjamin Edes, and John Gill. In the twentieth century, stalwart CBS newsman Walter Cronkite (often billed as "the most trusted man in America") at one point declared the war in Vietnam "unwinnable."

And before him, legendary CBS journalist Edward R. Murrow was calling upon
Americans to see Senator Joe McCarthy for the hoax he was in pressing slander-
ous claims against individuals and groups he labeled as communists. What seems
new, however, is that the kind of journalism that Dobbs and O'Reilly practice
(and O'Reilly's show is, admittedly, seen more as a commentary than Dobb's
news-formatted show) is done every single night. Their opinions are not the rare
ones slid into a frustrating news report, but are mixed in with regularity to the
facts their shows report. And since both of these news shows have done well in
the ratings, it is likely America will see more of this perspective.

    The Passionate Perspective. As I said earlier, this has been popularly dubbed
"emotional journalism," as its hallmark is usually a display of emotion by the
journalist covering the story. Whereas traditional journalists believe the hallmark of American journalism is emotional detachment from the story and the
people in it, the passionate perspective thrusts the journalist's emotions into
the story for a variety of reasons. Some journalists, for example, believe there is
nothing wrong with letting themselves feel what everyone else at the scene of
a tragedy is feeling. In fact, these journalists believe that in covering these stories
of emotion, it is important to understand what others are feeling at the scene.
They believe that ignoring or distancing themselves from emotions—when the
story is about emotions—is tantamount to missing the heart (no pun intended)
of the story. Other journalists believe it is foolhardy to believe that any journalist
could not be emotionally moved by a tragedy he or she is covering, so why not
be honest with yourself and place those emotions in context instead of denying
that they are there in the first place? And still others—like CNN's Anderson
Cooper—believe there is nothing wrong with showing an emotion like anger
to a source who seems to either be dismissive, obfuscating, or outright lying.
Anderson told CNN's Larry King in the summer of 2006 that he allowed
his anger to show in his year-long coverage of Hurricane Katrina because he
got tired of watching dead bodies float by him in the street while politicians
were complimenting each other for doing such a good job in responding to
the ensuing flood. At one point, in fact, Cooper interrupted Louisiana Sen.
Mary Landrieu as she was responding to his question about the cleanup in
New Orleans. Senator Landrieu was asking Cooper if he had heard about a measure Congress was pushing that might help, when Cooper abruptly interrupted
her and said, "Excuse me Senator. I haven't heard that because for the last four
days I've been standing here knee-deep in water and watching bodies float by."
He ended his outburst by asking her, "Do you get the anger that these people
here are feeling?" Explaining his angry reaction to the senator, Cooper told King
he tries never to be rude, but that he feels it is his job to get "answers" instead of
"responses" from government officials. He said if he has to get angry to get a real
answer—and to possibly get relief for the victims—then he sometimes gets
angry. Cooper said he doesn't believe in taking sides or "wearing my politics on
my sleeve." But he does believe in trying to get help for the helpless. Implicit
in Cooper's responses to King, especially when he noted that "I made a promise"

to the residents of New Orleans to stay on the story until they got help, that he considers part of his role to be advocate for the victims of tragedies, victims who probably cannot get the help they need themselves from the government.[10]

COMMUNITY VERSUS METRO MEDIA

It would be incorrect to assume that a story's credibility is related solely to the size of the news operation that produced it. Just because large newspapers or television networks have more editors and producers than smaller ones, it doesn't always follow that a large operation will get the story right and a smaller one will get it wrong. A lot more news copy flows through a larger newspaper than a smaller one on a daily basis. So smaller papers can usually get by with fewer editors. Also, local media know their communities better than larger media operations, which are often stationed many miles away. In fact, when reporters from a network or out-of-town newspaper come to a local community to do a story, they often begin by interviewing the local editor or reporters. So the accuracy and the nuance of local media stories can often surpass those of out-of-town media who "parachute" in for a day or two to get a big story.

News consumers should understand, however, that a community newspaper or radio station has a special role to fulfill in addition to publishing or airing a news story. Community media are often a town's chief boosters, and they take extra care in being sensitive to local reputations and issues. Small-town America is a more close-knit environment than are the large cities and suburbs, and local journalists know they live among their friends and are more approachable with their store-front newspaper or radio operations. So, in a way, personal account-ability is a big concern for journalists working for community media. This special role can, at times, result in withholding certain information or writing about it in a way that demonstrates an understanding of the local sensitivities involved. A story that might be done in a big city might not be done in a smaller commu-nity, or it may be done in a different way. A couple examples of this are as follows:

In 1979, in a community of about 60,000 people in Montana, a daily news-paper was presented with the dilemma of a young woman's brutal murder. Unknown to the community, this woman who had excelled at school and in her personal life fell into prostitution in Washington, D.C. One night, the news-paper's editor received a call from the local funeral home informing him of her death and giving him information for an obituary. The editor also received a call from The Washington Post whose reporter wanted information about the young woman for a "fallen angel" story the Post planned to do in a couple days. The Post was read in this community and was available in street racks. The local editor's dilemma was (1) whether to run a front-page story himself on the murder of a local woman-turned prostitute in faraway Washington, and (2) if he ran it, how should he handle it? Knowing the victim's parents were living and teaching in the community and knowing the fondness townspeople had for the victim made his problem even greater. Yet, if he chose not to run it, how could he be true to his calling as a newsman? And would his readers trust a newspaper that turned away from a story like this, while a newspaper published a couple thousand miles away carried it on the streets of the girl's hometown? The editor decided to run an obituary on the front page of the newspaper which focused on the victim's accomplishments and positive contributions. Then, two days later on an inside page, he produced a full story on the woman's death, but emphasized again the positive aspects of her life and left out some of the more sensational quotes and details that the *Post* story had contained. When challenged by many in the community for running the story at all, he defended it as a warning to other teenaged girls in the community, since this victim was recruited in an area bar for her ill-fated stint at prostitution. He also noted that the story was not sensationalized in his paper as the community felt it had been in the *Post*.

A second example occurred in 2001 in an Oklahoma City suburb about the same size as the Montana community. This case also involved a tragic death of one of its young residents, albeit an accident which occurred on the Colorado ski slopes. Like the Montana woman, this teenaged boy was a stellar student and also a youth leader in his church. When the news reached the newspaper that he had died from a collision on a ski slope, the editor ran the story on the front page, and the community was in mourning. That same day, the editor discovered that the youth had been skiing on a borrowed ski pass, which in Colorado is technically a criminal offense, given the value of skiers to the companies running the ski trails. The next day the newspaper ran a front-page story on that and drew outrage from the community. The reaction was so strong that the newspaper eventually hosted a town forum at which its editors and staff interacted with leaders in the community about the ethics of that coverage. The newspaper defended the decision to run the story as newsworthy, yet its editors did agree that it could have been handled more sensitively.

Editors and producers often juggle the news value of a story with the projected impact it will have on the community and the fallout that may result from it. As a result, some self-censorship takes place by the news media, often to the surprise of many media critics who feel journalists always bare everything, no matter how distasteful. The old journalistic adage of "publish and be damned," and its companion thought, "it is the newspaper's job to print the news and raise hell," are more debated today by a more market-oriented news media than ever before in journalistic history. Some journalists still agree with those sentiments; some don't. News consumers who wonder why a newspaper or television station cover particular stories, tell them in particular ways, or back off on the coverage altogether, should consider the debates that take place among editors and between reporters.

Another reason big-city media handle some stories differently than smaller media is that criteria of news value may change between an urban news market and a rural one. The last chapter provided a laundry list of general criteria of news value, but it did not mention that smaller markets sometimes see news differently than the big markets. It makes sense, because a major criterion is what the reader or viewer is concerned with, or even fears. Dressed up in journalism books as the "psychological proximity" criterion of news value, essentially this refers to what interests people and why. For example, in a large city, people are often worried about crime. Some find themselves in the grip of fear that they might be the city's next crime victim; possibly at a local ATM, or standing in line in a bank to make a deposit, or just entering the wrong convenience store at the wrong time. Exacerbating that fear is the isolation and loneliness that many city dwellers feel, even though they live in the midst of a million other people. Not only might they die, but they might die alone with no one trying to stop it or no one caring, this idea goes. Because the fear of crime is so big in some cities, news consumers might be drawn more to stories about crime in their city as they use these stories to orient them to the location and timing of the threats so they can avoid them. Communication scholars would say this is an example of the *surveillance* use that a reader or viewer might use the media for. Others would just say we often use media stories as a roadmap to orient ourselves to the threats—as well as opportunities—of our cities.

In rural areas, however, the threat of crime is very low, hence news consumers don't want to feed on a steady diet of crime news. Their minds are on other things; sometimes other kinds of threats (like drought for farmers), but more often on the placid aspects of community living. Therefore, community news-papers tend to emphasize more people-oriented news, advance stories on upcoming community events, stories of progress in the town, and always names, names, and more names. It's not that community media avoid tragedies when they occur, it's just that they write about the things their news consumers are interested in. And those things don't usually include the fear of local crime.

FACTUAL AND CONTEXTUAL ACCURACY

When readers or viewers ponder the accuracy of news or feature stories, they should understand that there are at least two kinds of such accuracy: factual and contextual. Factual accuracy covers a broad spectrum from the spelling of names, the correctness of ages, titles, and addresses, to the account of the inci-dent itself and the characterization of those individuals involved in—or affected by—that incident or issue. Contextual accuracy covers an even broader spectrum and concerns the completed puzzle the reporter assembles from the various facts. Sometimes a reporter can have the right facts but the wrong completed puzzle; factual accuracy is in place, but contextual accuracy is not. Sometimes contextual accuracy may be a matter of emphasis or story slant or angle. An example of this could include the Montana daily described earlier, whose editor chose to avoid the "fallen angel" aspect of the young woman's death and instead emphasize her positive achievements and contributions to the community.

Many reporters feel that most of the attacks on their work by readers or viewers are of the contextual accuracy variety. It is a more subjective playing field where both sides can have a better chance of making their cases than if arguing over whether a crime victim is 18 or 19 years old. Sometimes the critiques are valid; sometimes reporters do get the larger truth wrong despite the accuracy of the facts underlying that depiction. What both sides of the debate are discussing is the *interpretation* which the reporter devises from the facts. Regarded by some inside the journalistic community and many outside it as beyond the journalist's role, interpretation is nevertheless an inevitable part of reporting. It can be extremely valid as well, depending on how discerning the reporter is and how gifted at obtaining the missing pieces needed for the finished puzzle. Journalists interpret all the time, and what's in question is not that they do it but how well they do it. Stringing facts together to form a story is what journalists do. They emphasize this or that; they define even basic ideas such as "tall" or "heavy" on the basis of the kind of height or weight they think bespeak those categories.

Most interpretation is not this simple, however, nor is it based on generally-accepted standards. Most journalistic interpretation involves interpreting one fact in light of another. It is moving toward the unknown on the basis of the known. The best interpretation is built on the back of a solid set of facts, hopefully coming from a variety of sources. Verification helps confirm the facts, and slowly these facts start revealing a larger picture or trend. Assembling these facts, triangulating them from different sources, and observing the picture that emerges from them are the essence of interpretation.

News consumers should remember that interpretation is *not* editorializing. The former is a matter of putting the right puzzle pieces together to form a correct picture; the latter is a matter of casting judgments on—or making value statements about —those pieces and/or the finished picture. And the latter does not belong in the news pages but on the opinion and editorial pages. In his book, *Understanding Global News*, Jaap van Ginneken captures some of the challenge that journalists face in using interpretive language in their stories:

> In our common-sense and everyday life, we consider language a simple instrument for the neutral reflection, the mirroring of the world. But is this realistic? Is there not always more than one synonym at hand, with a slightly different connotation? Is not the use of euphemisms and metaphors commonplace, particularly by influential spokesmen or women. and even if journalists themselves strive for unambiguous language, is this an attainable ideal? How can evaluations become imperceptibly woven into descriptions, through various ordinary means of sentence formulation and narrative construction?[11]

WHAT STORY STRUCTURE MAY REVEAL

Another clue into the design and effect of news and feature stories can be found in the way the journalist structures them. This subject was broached earlier when we discussed the framing of news. Story structure or formatting can say a lot about what the reporter is intending to do and how he or she perceives the story in the first place. Print journalists use a variation of two different storytelling structures: the inverted pyramid and the narrative. Television journalists use a variant of these as well, but most will add a sense of immediacy with more use of present-tense verbs, and will try to address early in the story the viewer's rhetorical question, "What's in it for me?" Let's take a look at these story structures and what they might reveal.

All journalists start from the premise that, in an age of intense media competition and the many ways in which people can spend their leisure time, it is very hard to get someone to read or watch your news story. The traditional story structure designed to address that reality is the inverted pyramid. It is called this because it begins not with the narrow details that define a narrative style of writing, but with the broad conclusion that the narrator builds up to. So a story about a police shootout following a bank robbery might begin: "Two men armed with automatic weapons died in a hail of gunfire with a dozen police officers outside the First National Bank today." The inverted pyramid is meant to emphasize the incident itself, and most such leads (the first paragraph of a news story) begin by stating who did what, when, or what was done to whom, when. The story then moves on to detail the incident, building from most interesting to least interesting points, or simply moving chronologically as the body of the above story might do. The inverted pyramid has no formal conclusion and just ends with what the reporter considers the least interesting details, just as it began with what he or she considered the most interesting or important.

The inverted pyramid is meant to catch the reader's attention with a sharp lead that delivers a quick summary of the action. The feeling is that if this can't be done, the reader will move on to another story or another diversion altogether. If, however, the reader does move on, then at least she or he has gotten the summary of the event. This story structure was first devised during the Civil War, when the Union war correspondents reporting from the South feared their telegraphed story transmissions might be cut off in mid-story by the wire snippers of Confederate soldiers. But the inverted pyramid outlasted that war and came to be the standard fare for journalism and is still used today. This structure lends itself best to breaking news stories, and it is largely predicated on the belief that the readers or viewers have not heard about this story yet. In the inverted pyramid format, the writer relies upon the action itself to engage the reader rather than a deftly-crafted narrative opening that either carefully describes the scene or an individual actor within the drama. At issue—especially in major stories—is the premise that the reader would not have already heard about the event through a plethora of newer media forms ranging from television to the Internet. And that reality has been driving print journalists more into the narrative storytelling structure than ever before.

A journalist doesn't have to attend many writing seminars, conventions of journalists, or professional development programs before realizing that the idea of narrative storytelling is very much in vogue these days as a journalistic style and structure. The narrative turns the inverted pyramid upside down, starting with details and working forward toward an eventual conclusion, just as a novelist would. It is a style that has been around for a while, and it first came to widespread use with writers like Truman Capote and Tom Wolfe in the 1960s. Originally dubbed the "new journalism," it has evolved into "literary journalism," and it values the way the story is told almost as much as the facts themselves. The hallmarks of this story structure include the following:

- An anecdotal or scene-setting opening instead of a summary lead. This lead focuses on an individual character or characters within the story or details the setting of the story vividly.

- The body of the story can go in one of several directions. The two most common forms are the following: (1) it can stay with the narrative all the way through the story, going to rising action, climax, and denouement just as a novelist would, or (2) it can shift from the opening narrative to a discussion of the larger issue. If it does this, then the writer employs a "nut" paragraph, which bolts the opening narrative to the exposition of the larger issue which the opener represents.

- Key elements in this narrative or semi-narrative style include a kind of "social autopsy" of the scene, a good amount of dialogue between characters in the story, a study of the most minute nonverbal cues of these characters, and a fair amount of subjective impression, especially in personality profiles or other feature stories.

Writers who follow this narrative format for many of their stories believe it brings a greater sense of realism and more visual qualities to a story that better enable the reader to "see" what the reporter sees and "hear" what she hears. In short, a well-crafted narrative story can be effective in transporting the reader or viewer to the scene that the reporter has witnessed. And, for most journalists, that is a supreme goal of their writing in the first place.

A note of caution is worthwhile about this narrative format, which focuses often on the individual as a type or representative of a larger group of people who face similar challenges or opportunities. Although this kind of focus and format breaks down an impersonal issue to one that is very personal, the individual it focuses on may—or may not be—exactly typical of others caught up in (or affected by) this issue or event. Politicians and government officials sometimes rebuke journalists for presenting persons they believe are not representative of the larger group the story focuses on. A related critique is that this form of storytelling is more emotional in tone, and politicians may argue that many issues need to be confronted rationally and not emotionally. Therefore, the critique goes, these stories don't represent the reality that everyone is facing. The ironic thing is that when politicians are giving speeches, they often resort to the same kinds of anecdotes and mean them to stand for larger groups of people. And they mean to go for the emotional jugular of their audiences.

Van Ginneken also notes the effect that *compression* has on the telling of a story. Clearly, on both television and in newspapers, stories must be compressed to fit the time and space available.[12] While space is virtually unlimited online, there are still pragmatic considerations that dictate stories not run too long. Readers don't particularly enjoy scrolling down reams of copy, and having journalists produce long stories is a costly business. If a story is told in the inverted pyramid style, more emphasis is usually placed on the who, what, when, and where. But the hardest challenge of any story—and the story part which takes the longest to explain—is the answer to the question of why it happened. Therefore, the why and sometimes the how get brief treatment in a traditional news story. Compression is the order of the day in television news, where few stories run longer than 90 seconds. British reporter Martin Bell wrote in his memoirs that the BBC often required him to use no more than a hundred seconds each night in telling the story of the war in Bosnia.

Van Ginneken also writes of "myths" that he believes are part of the news story process and outcome. He quotes John Fiske as describing myths as follows:

> A myth is a story by which a culture explains or understands some aspect of reality or nature. Primitive myths are about life and death, men and gods, good and evil. Our sophisticated myths are about masculinity, and femininity, about the family, about success, about the British policeman, about science. A myth, for Barthes, is a culture's way of thinking about something, a way of conceptualizing or understanding it. Barthes thinks of a myth as a chain of related concepts. Thus the traditional myth of the British policeman includes concepts of friendliness, reassurance, solidarity, non-aggressiveness, lack of firearms.[13]

EDITORIALIZING IN NEWS STORIES

The late semanticist, college president, and U.S. senator S.I. Hayakawa wrote a significant book for all writers. Called *Language in Thought and Action*, Hayakawa's book detailed the different types and uses of language in America and discussed how they affect what people think and how they behave. Hayakawa recognized three broad types of language, which he called reports, inferences, and judgments. Report language is the most neutral, fact-based language, while inferences inject interpretation (describing the unknown on the basis of the known) and judgments make value statements and deliver opinions. As was mentioned earlier, readers and viewers often tend to confuse inferences with judgments, and they really are not the same thing; at least they don't have to be. An inference might be a simple process of uniting two related facts (such as a large number of absences by a senator from voting sessions and a speech by that senator underscoring the importance of attendance at those sessions).

Connecting those two puzzle pieces together would suggest to the reporter that the senator has trouble walking his talk. Judgment language (editorializing) would seep in if the reporter were to add an unattributed comment such as, "The senator should attend more voting sessions." This is an opinion and does not belong in a news story.

While beginning college journalism students often make such crossovers (some of them seemingly innocent as in "We should all respect our president"), professional journalists understand this crossover is unacceptable in the news pages or in a newscast. Between print and television, these judgments are probably seen more on television than in newspapers. The place where such judgments (often in the form of reporter speculation) occur most often are in the reporter "stand-ups." These are the sections of TV stories where the reporter stands in front of the camera often at the end of the piece to wrap it up and speculate on what will happen next or "place the story in context." Viewers should recognize such statements for what they are: not a part of the facts of the story, but an impression or judgment of the reporter.

SUMMARY

There are several things any news consumer can look for in evaluating news and feature stories in print or on the air. One of those clues is the journalist himself or herself; the more a reader or viewer understands the motivations and challenges of journalists, the better they can understand the stories they produce. Sometimes a deciding factor on how news is presented results from whether it occurs in a larger or smaller media market. Sometimes news is judged differently in each kind of market, as smaller media tend to consider issues of sensitivity toward their readers more than metro media might. Also, the issues and fears of readers and viewers in metro markets differ from those in rural markets. The story structure used can also be a clue to the intent and the nature of the story. Stories told in the inverted pyramid convey one impression; stories done in the narrative convey another. News consumers should also judge whether they are focusing on factual accuracy or contextual accuracy as they critique stories. And, finally, consumers should understand the different types of language available to the reporter: reports, inferences, and judgments. The first form tends to be dry and often gives way to inferences, while judgments should be reserved for the editorial page.

CHAPTER 7

Politicians and Journalists: A Symbiotic Relationship

In America, name recognition counts in politics, and it counts for a lot if one wants to get elected. What are the odds, for example, that Arnold Schwarzenegger would have been elected governor of California were it not for his instant name recognition courtesy of his celebrity status? Certainly the same thing helped propel Ronald Reagan into the California governor's mansion. Jesse Ventura's recognition as a professional wrestler helped him take that state's highest office, and—years earlier—Bill Bradley's celebrity status as a professional basketball player helped him take a seat in the U.S. Senate from New Jersey. Congressman Jack Kemp had achieved status as a professional football player, and the list goes on and on. Politicians hate it when they go up against people like these who already have that name recognition from their former life in the movies or in professional athletics. That same name recognition takes a relatively unknown candidate years and a lot of money to achieve. Some must feel they have to expend an enormous amount of money and energy just to get to the starting gate of an election.

MANY WAYS TO GET THERE

Most political candidates don't have the built-in name recognition that celebrities have, so they have to become adept at getting the media to cover them, and to cover them regularly. Without media coverage, a candidacy is dead

in the water for state and national elections. With it, the hopeful stands a fighting chance. Sometimes that name recognition comes from former positions the
candidate may have held. Perhaps he was a police chief; perhaps he was a fire
chief who delivered hourly press briefings during a disaster that occurred in
his city. Such was the case with Assistant Fire Chief Jon Hansen of Oklahoma
City, who became a media celebrity from his tireless work as spokesman for the
search-and-rescue efforts in the days and weeks following the bombing of the
Murrah Federal Building in April of 1995. Perhaps a woman has achieved status
as an intrepid assistant district attorney, prosecuting several high-profile cases
and appearing regularly on TV news and in the newspapers for her interviews
and press conferences. Perhaps someone like that becomes a Nancy Grace and
winds up achieving even greater celebrity status by hosting her own local or
cable television shows. Perhaps the politician is a former high-profile defense
lawyer who—like the ADA—is a regular on television news and talk shows
about crime and criminals. Or perhaps the candidate had the help of a public
relations team of media trainers, like the Indianapolis firm of Lee/Willis
Communications, Inc., in grooming their image for the media.

Whatever way a candidate achieves name recognition, the result is often
the same: he or she becomes a person very hard to beat come election time.
And the role of the news media is obvious in the creation of that celebrity
candidate. Currying favor with journalists is an important part of any politician's
strategy. In some ways, maybe the most important part.

THE MAKING OF A MEDIA DARLING

In a 2008 presidential race that has featured entrenched presumed candidates
with high name recognition like Hillary Clinton, Al Gore, and John McCain,
what chance was there for a national unknown to take center-stage in the
national media in 2006 when speculation went into high gear over possible
presidential hopefuls? When it came to Democratic Illinois Senator Barack
Obama, the chances were very good. Within a span of months, this first-term
U.S. senator was grabbing the cover of *Time* magazine (October 23, 2006) and
being featured and touted as a presidential hopeful in high-profile network and
cable newscasts and political talk shows like *Meet the Press* and the immensely
popular *Oprah Winfrey Show*. For most Americans, the name Barack Obama
had never been spoken prior to October 2006. Within a month or two, it was a
name on the lips of all political insiders and many of the nation's voters. Can this
happen without the help of the national media? Clearly not. Yet why should the
nation's political journalists stand up and take notice simultaneously of this
virtual political unknown who has the seeming political misfortune to have the
middle name of Hussein?

Part of the answer is found in the man himself, and part in the needs of
the news media and the criteria by which news is judged. Barack Hussein

Obama, Jr. was 46 years old when he began grabbing the national spotlight in the fall of 2006. Two years earlier he had won the U.S. Senate seat vacated by Peter Fitzgerald in Illinois. His Republican opponent, Jack Ryan, withdrew from the race amid a personal scandal, and he was hastily replaced by Alan Keyes. The Republican turmoil resulted in a landslide victory for Obama, who became the only African American to hold a U.S. Senate seat at that time. During that campaign, the Democrats saw a rising star and asked Obama to deliver the key-note address at the 2004 Democratic National Convention, which he did. This keynote address, a high point of national media coverage at these conventions, has often thrust virtual unknowns into the media spotlight. While still in his first year of office, Obama was being asked by reporters if he planned to seek the presidency in 2008. By mid-term election time in the fall of 2006, the national media were widely portraying him as a presidential candidate and noting that Hillary Clinton's presumed run for the White House could be derailed by Obama. In the winter of 2007, he made it official that he would seek the nomination.

Earlier in this book the criteria of news value were laid out, and it is interesting to note how some of the more important criteria intersect with this man Barack Obama:

Uniqueness. Certainly Obama fits this criterion. He was the only African American U.S. senator at the time of his election, and he won as a Democrat in 2004 when Republican candidates were sweeping national offices. When he took office, he was ranked next to last in seniority among the 100 U.S. senators, yet the next year Time magazine named him one of "the world's most influential people" in its annual edition spotlighting 100 "leaders and revolutionaries." Clearly, here was a politician who was now on the radar of the national media.

Human Interest. Obama's youthfulness and handsome good looks, coupled with his confident on-camera persona and ability to laugh, go together to cause this man to connect with the public. And the fact he was born to racially mixed parents, came from a middle-class beginning, and lived through his parents' divorce cause even a wider array of Americans to relate well with him.

Rugged Individualism. One of the strongest of the criteria of news value is depicted in the person who dares to defy the odds and fights the good fight. Again, Barack Obama fits this criterion. His never-say-die attitude helped him rise as he was being shuffled from parents to grandparents, and from place to place, and eventually to graduate magna cum laude from Harvard Law School. Like the Rev. Jesse Jackson, he pushed for continuation of the civil rights strug-gle, and won the admiration of many in Illinois.

Moderatism. Barack Obama, while African American and a Democrat, is a man who has shown to reach out to all groups and sides and do it in a way which doesn't come across as radical. His attitude was seen in a portion of his 2004 keynote address at the Democratic National Convention when he said:

> The pundits like to slice-and-dice our country into Red State and Blue States; Red States for Republicans, Blue States for Democrats. But I've got news for them,

too. We worship an awesome God in the Blue States, and we don't like federal agents poking around our libraries in the Red States. We coach Little League in the Blue States and have gay friends in the Red States. There are patriots who opposed the war in Iraq and patriots who supported it. We are one people, all of us pledging allegiance to the stars and stripes, all of us defending the United States of America.[1]

Leadership. Although a freshman senator with relatively little power to wield in Washington, the national media has seen in Obama the qualities of a leader it believes will continue to surface to make this politician a force on the national stage and a potential candidate for the presidency. Of course, the people making this decision to provide a brighter and wider spotlight for a candidate who had little popular name recognition among the nation's voters are journalists themselves. They may be guided by their knowledge of history as they look to the kinds of people who became national leaders, and they may be guided by Gallup and Roper polls in making this determination. The latter influence begs the question, however, of whether the polls guide the media or whether the media—by their coverage—help determine the results of the polls. Clearly the national media have hordes of politicians to choose from as they cast about for the individuals they think have the best chances of challenging for national office. It would not be uncommon for a relative unknown to believe he or she had won the lottery should they be the recipient of such media attention that catapults their chances even higher toward winning their campaigns.

IT'S NOT ONE-SIDED

The equation between politicians and the media is not one-sided, however. The media need the politicians as well. One only has to look at the relative importance of the state and national news beats to understand why. As journalists rank them, the most important and prestigious of the journalistic beats are the White House and Congress at the national level, and the governor and legislature at the state level. Network and cable news correspondents aspire to become White House correspondent, the ultimate news beat in the nation's capital. Everything else seems to pale in comparison. As it often happens, the network or cable correspondent whose assigned candidate wins the presidential race is assigned as White House correspondent for that news operation for the duration of that Administration. So, in a real sense, the correspondent has a personal career stake in her or his candidate winning office. One star might well rise with the other. It makes sense, too, for what other reporter would have come to know that presidential candidate as well as the reporter who has been assigned to cover him or her over the past year or more? Further, knowing that a reporter might become the network's White House correspondent is a force that keeps her batteries charged during the long months of chasing that candidate around the country during the campaign.

Veteran CBS journalist Bob Schieffer, a former White House correspondent, explains the job this way:

> Covering the White House is the most glamorous job in all of journalism, and in television, the most prestigious. It is the place where the networks assign reporters who have been put on the fast track, the testing ground for future stars, and it is the White House correspondent who generally gets more air time on the Evening News programs than all of the other reporters, but I soon learned what other White House reporters knew: It was not always as exciting as it seemed from the outside and could sometimes be downright boring, a place where real reporting was sometimes all but impossible and where you had contact with the president and his staff only when they choose to see you.[2]

Politics has built-in drama at many levels, and drama is what pulls readers and viewers into stories. Not only is there the drama of a close election campaign, but there is the drama of the theater of politics itself. Count the number of political talk shows on television, realize that the three top Sunday morning shows (Meet the Press, Face the Nation, and This Week) are nearly always focused on politics, and you see the importance of politics to the American public. Were it not so, these talk shows would be focusing on something else entirely. In America, politics, sports, and entertainment sell. And it is often hard to tell which sells most; possibly because the three are intertwined in the theme of winning and losing. The big story in entertainment every Monday is which film blew the opposition away at the box office over the weekend. Not only are they all connected around theme, but also around metaphors used to describe the battles. We have "horse-race" coverage of politics, a candidate's "dropping the ball" or "scoring a home run," or a presidential media aide like Michael Deaver referring to the creation of Regan's campaign commercials as "making little movies."

Suffice it to say that politicians need journalists as much as journalists need politicians. That is especially so in this age of 24-hour news channels and deadline-every-second Internet news sites. Former CNN newsman Mike Boettcher has observed about the ravenous appetite of 24-hour news networks, "The beast must be fed, and it must be fed on a regular basis."[3] In a democratic society where elections are so important, politicians become important to the media, and airtime becomes vital to politicians.

FROM A PARTISAN PRESS ERA

Today's journalists do business in an age where most mainstream media attempt to take a neutral political stance, at least on the news pages or in the newscast. This has not always been the case in American history, however, as we will discuss in a moment. Today, however, nowhere is the ideal of objectivity more important than in news stories about candidates for office and the election campaigns themselves. Even if a newspaper takes a political stand on its editorial page, the idea is that the news pages are off-limits to partisanship or bias. That works fairly well on most news staffs, although sometimes a reader might detect some bias in the kinds of issues the newspaper deems important to report. For example, one metro daily might be very conservative when it comes to government welfare programs, seeing them as a waste of the public's money. So there may be a sense in the newsroom that stories about welfare programs will receive more space, especially if it can be proven that those programs that don't seem to work out as planned. Such was the case at one newspaper with which I was attached, and it so happened that the newspaper was one of the more politically conservative newspapers in the nation. In large measure, however, the news pages are separated from the editorial pages in philosophy. It is no coincidence that they are also separated physically at large newspapers where the newsroom is on one floor and the editorial writers work on another floor.

Shortly after the Revolutionary War, however, when America was testing its democratic wings at the end of the eighteenth century, this country entered into a rather dark era of partisan journalism. This was the time before any mass media were developed in America, and the media landscape consisted of many smaller newspapers geared often to politics and business. Lacking any independent financial base such as the media enjoy today, the newspaper editors accepted grants and subsidies from political parties; indeed, some newspapers were begun primarily as propaganda sheets for a particular party. Examples included the *Gazette of the United States*, generally viewed as the outstanding Federalist Party newspaper in the late eighteenth century. Sponsored and supported by Alexander Hamilton, leader of the Federalists, this newspaper was edited by John Fenno, who issued the first edition on April 15, 1789. Another strong Federalist voice was that of Noah Webster, usually associated with his dictionary more than politics. But he was also seen in his time as a great editor of the daily *Minerva* and the semiweekly newspaper, the *Herald*. On the Anti-Federalist side was Philip Freneau, known as "Jefferson's editor,"[4] who began as editor of the *National Gazette* in 1791 and whose editorial battles with John Fenno were famous at the time. Although these newspapers were seen as good ones for the era, there was often little pretense at objectivity among the partisan papers, and it was understood that they were promoting the candidates and the causes of the party that underwrote them financially.

From a pluralistic standpoint, the one bright thing that can be said of this otherwise dark journalistic era is that there were so many of these partisan papers representing different political interests that a reader could get both sides by simply reading newspapers from each party. In some ways, it was more of an era of plurality than America enjoys today, at least among its newspapers.

Today there is generally one daily newspaper serving any city, large or small. If that newspaper takes a political stand on its editorial page, there may be no countering voice unless it is a smaller, often more specialized newspaper doing business in the city. A common phenomenon in large American cities is to have the one metro daily (a few cities like New York, Boston, and Chicago still have two, however) and a so-called "alternative weekly" newspaper. This second newspaper gets its name from the fact it offers an alternative political viewpoint to the metro daily. These alternative weeklies generally focus on two kinds of news: politics and the arts. Examples of them are the *Riverfront Times* in St. Louis, *Boston Phoenix*, *Memphis Flyer*, and the *Observer* in Dallas. They attempt to provide some plurality of viewpoint, but their readership often pales in comparison to the dominant metro daily in the city.

What proved to be the undoing of the era of the partisan press was not outrage among readers yearning for more objectivity. Instead, the undoing factor was the emergence of the mass-circulation daily newspaper in the 1830s and 1840s. When publisher Benjamin Day began selling his New York Sun for a penny an issue and redefining news as anything which would interest the common New Yorker, the door was flung open wide for the modern-day newspaper. Along with general-interest news, often told in a flamboyant style, came a large general-interest readership. And along with the larger readership came a new and more independent way of financing the newspaper: advertising.

Ironically, while many critics see advertising as a challenge to editorial freedom, it has proven to be the opposite in most cases. Advertisers don't particularly care about political viewpoints; they care about getting the largest number of readers brought to bear on their ads. In order to achieve large circulations, newspaper publishers discovered that they had to be more nonpartisan in their news columns so they wouldn't alienate large and important chunks of readership. They might offer opinions on their editorial pages, but the news columns were for news stories. As newspapers grew in size and influence, political candidates of opposing parties began placing ads in the same paper, further underscoring the need for the newspaper to keep its news as free of political partisanship as possible. Thus, for all intents and purposes, the "dark age of journalism" came to an end with the emergence of the mass-circulation daily newspaper which, besides books, proved to be America's first kind of mass medium.

HOW THE DANCE WORKS

It is interesting to study the dance between journalists and politicians and to see how each works to manipulate the other into achieving its different goals, which sometimes don't seem so different. Usually the goal of a politician is to get elected or to get re-elected, making himself or herself look good in the process. Usually the goal of a journalist is to obtain material for a good story and, hopefully in the process, convey a piece of truth to her readers or viewers. Anyone who has seen episodes of television's *West Wing* gets a glimpse into how this jockeying between politicians and journalists occurs at the level of the federal government, and of the important role the White House press office plays in the process. Press aides to the president are among some of the smartest, most creative, and most energetic professionals in Washington. Often they come from the ranks of working journalists and/or from the ranks of professional public relations practitioners. They understand the media and their needs, they understand the psyche of journalists, and they understand how the media define news. With that understanding and a very deep set of financial resources, these public relations professionals who work for the government can be a daunting force for journalists to contend with. For example, the best of the White House press officers are proactive and swing into action before a story breaks. They sniff out the possible issues and events which might make the evening news, and they set up in advance to deal with the inevitable questions that will come their way. They put the president into pleasing photo opportunities and often use those "photo ops" to counter negative news stories that the media may be developing for the day. An example of how this works was outlined in a PBS interview with journalist Bill Moyers as Michael Deaver, former media aide to President Reagan, explained a typical day of reacting to negative news.[5]

Deaver said the White House press office knew a government report was coming out the next day that showed housing starts were down around the country. Since housing starts are a primary index of the nation's economy, and since a negative story on the economy reflects badly on the White House, Deaver said he knew he had to be proactive in the administration's response. That response a counter-offensive aimed at distracting the public from the real issue of negative housing starts. Deaver used the photo-op as his means. The next morning President Reagan was put onto Air Force One for a flight to Fort Worth. There he donned a hard hat and toured a new subdivision that was going up. The houses were still in the framing stages, and here was the president of the United States walking through the partially-completed structures. This was the video that the networks used over the audio about the nation's housing starts being down. Deaver said a White House poll conducted later that evening showed many American viewers had picked up an entirely different message from watching the video of the president in the framed-out houses. That message was, ironically, that housing starts must be up; not down.

On another occasion, the White House knew a story was coming out about a tax break to corporations. Since that type of story usually aggravates many in America's middle class, the White House put Reagan on a plane and flew him to Boston, where he was taken to an Irish working-class pub to hoist beers with the locals. Again, this video played over the corporation story, and the visual message from it was that the president is just one of the guys.

From these experiences and others, Deaver said he came to believe that, in the battle between the eye and the ear, the eye wins every time when it comes to viewers watching television. In more cases than not, he explained, the video drowns out the audio and can actually produce a totally different message in the minds of the viewers.

The challenge for presidential press secretaries is daunting, as the career of Mike McCurry, former press secretary for President Clinton, shows. McCurry was a bit of an anomaly among press secretaries in that he had the respect of most

White House journalists and managed to mingle with them socially while still representing the interests of the president. His struggle was the one faced by all White House press spokespersons: to achieve and maintain credibility with both the president and the news media and somehow serve as a conduit between the two entities. Washington journalist Howard Kurtz explained it this way:

> Each day, it seemed, McCurry faced a moral dilemma. He stood squarely at the intersection of news and propaganda, in the white-hot glare of the media spotlight, the buffer between self-serving administration officials and a cynical pack of reporters. The three principles of his job, he believed, were telling the truth, giving people a window on the White House, and protecting the president, but the last imperative often made the first two difficult. If the corporate spokesman for Exxon or General Motors stretched the truth on occasion, well that was seen as part of the job... [but] more was expected of the presidential press secretary, whose every syllable was transcribed by news agencies...McCurry found himself facing the question that had dogged every presidential rpess secretary since the Nixon administration: whether it is possible to tell the truth, or something approximating the truth.[6]

But the press secretary (a title which has given way more to "spokesperson") is only the most visible of the minions of White House press officers. Each White House has another important position known as communication director. Under Clinton, Don Baer held that job. He had a different philosophy than many who have occupied his office: he didn't necessarily believe the White House should get so focused on—or paranoid about—the next day's television story or headlines. He also differed somewhat from Michael Deaver's belief that pictures were more important than words on television. Baer knew he had, in Clinton, a master public speaker and a pretty good communicator one-on-one as well. So Baer developed a belief that what Clinton said was more effective than what others might be saying about him. In a real way he saw President Clinton as staging his own private conversation with Americans, apart from the one the journalists themselves were staging. He developed an analogy between White House journalists and movie critics: a newspaper's critic might give a movie a bad review, but often moviegoers loved it anyway and turned it into a box-office hit. Hollywood is littered with success stories that critics had panned. So why shouldn't it work this way in the White House? If Clinton gave a great performance that resonated with the public, what difference does it make if journalists didn't like it? After all, journalists are not the most popular professionals in America.

Kurtz provides an example of how this phenomenon worked in the Clinton White House.[7] One time Clinton revealed his plan for HOPE scholarships, a program designed to provide parents of college students tax credits of as much as $1,500. Although the reaction from the Washington press was cynical and was perceived as a manipulative tactic to gain support among the American middle class, the public seemed to perceive Clinton as genuinely concerned about their kids' chances of going to college. White House polls also showed the public felt he wanted to help them out with those tuition bills. So they liked Clinton and his message, and tuned out the critiques.

Another viewpoint on the Washington press came from Rahm Emanuel, special assistant to the president. Emanuel believed the media functioned within models, which he felt were tidy belief systems that largely reflected elite opinion. He dismissed the notion of objective reporting and felt Washington journalists were heavily biased. This notion came from a Democrat in the White House and not a Republican, countering a popular belief among conservatives that the press is only out to "get" Republican presidents. President Carter's press secretary, Jody Powell, encountered the same animosity from the press in that Democratic administration. To Emanuel, Washington journalists had a preconception of Clinton as what Kurtz called, "a petulant little child with an uncontrollable appetite."[8]

Emanuel believed wholeheartedly that was not an apt description of Bill Clinton, who he saw as having his hand on the pulse of what Americans really wanted. So Emanuel positioned himself as a kind of radar for the president, often phoning the network newsrooms at 10:05 a.m. each morning, just after their morning news briefings, to find out what they were working on and—hopefully—to debunk what he felt might be false reports. As Kurtz articulates:

> He understood the rhythms of the beast...Often, Emanuel felt, the prevailing media paradigms worked in the administration's favor. He had been a chief strategist in helping to pass the 1994 ban on assault weapons, and there the [media's] paradigm was clear: gun control good, opponents NRA stooges...Journalists simply failed to appreciate how their deeply held views shaped their coverage. But it was this same self-absorption that caused many reporters to dismiss much of Clinton's agenda as small-bore. Take the Family and Medical Leave Act. It wasn't a big deal for a hot-shot journalist to take time off from work if his or her kid was sick, but for a factory worker in Illinois, the new law was a godsend...There were two conversations going on in the country—the daily chatter between reporters and political operatives over all the maneuvering and minutiae, and the president's attempt to talk to the masses about the real issues in their lives...Emanuel believed that by mastering the second conversation, Clinton could effectively neutralize the first.[9]

SUMMARY

In politics, name recognition probably counts for more than any other single element in an election campaign. Therefore, politicians go to great lengths to get that recognition with the public, and they know they have to go through the media to get it. That means they must curry favor with journalists, craft unique images of themselves that have a chance to stand out among the competition, and stage unique events to draw media coverage. It is getting harder and harder to be unique, however, in an age of saturation media coverage where the public seems to have heard and seen just about everything. The "dance" between politicians and journalists is not one-sided, however, as journalists wind up needing politicians, too. For a political journalist, it is essential he or she has good relationships with politicians and officeholders, and that these people provide them with good, usable stories on a regular basis. So the symbiotic relationship between press and politicians lives on, despite the fact that one of the chief roles of journalists is to serve as an adversarial watchdog on the government and its leaders. It puts both journalists and politicians in positions of tension. The case of Barack Obama provides an interesting lesson in the creation of a "media darling," as the national media made this Illinois politician a household name in 2006. The higher a candidate rates on established criteria of news value, the higher his or her chances of becoming a household name. It is also interesting to peek inside the White House and see the challenges faced by the White House Press Office and, particularly, the president's press secretary or spokesperson. This individual must juggle three different roles at once, and the truth-telling role is the one hardest to pull off at times. Finally, for our purposes, the question arises of what kinds—if any—of "paradigms" do the media operate within; what are the pervasive beliefs and values of Washington journalists? And a related question is how are their news reports framed by these paradigms, if at all?

CHAPTER 8

Presidents and the Press

As the last chapter came to a close, we broached the subject of how the White House deals with the Washington Press Corps. This chapter will look in more depth at how some individual presidents have interfaced with the nation's media, what they thought about the press, and how their presidencies survived in the face of extreme media scrutiny. Although several differences in media relations have surfaced among the 43 presidents through George W. Bush, all presidents have at least one thing in common: they have all felt the sting of the media spotlight as well as its glow during their years in the White House. And even those like Thomas Jefferson, who have been staunch supporters of press freedom, have still critiqued the media's White House coverage on occasion. We'll begin this chapter with a look at a few well-placed quips about the media and individual journalists from some of these presidents.

A FEW PRESIDENTIAL ZINGERS

Among a few of the more interesting quips presidents have made about the press over the years have been the following:

- Thomas Jefferson, usually quoted for a statement he made on the importance of journalism in a democracy, also once noted, "I do not take a single newspaper, nor read one a month and I feel myself infinitely the happier for it."[1]
- Dan Rather tells the following story about a time in 1955 when Lyndon Johnson, then Senate majority leader, grabbed the phone out of his hand at LBJ's Texas ranch. Rather had been talking to his producer at a Houston television station.

Johnson, angered with Rather, yelled into the receiver, "This is Lyndon Johnson. I don't know who the hell you are, and I damned well don't know who this rude pissant is. But I can tell you this: He doesn't belong here, I'm throwing his ass out, what he just told you is bullshit and if you use it, I'll sue you." A short time later Lady Bird Johnson saw Rather on the road and yelled from her lowered car window, "Whatever he said, he didn't mean anything by it, honey. It's just his way."[2]

- President Woodrow Wilson became outraged when newspaper reporters speculated that his daughter planned to marry soon. Wilson lashed out at reporters saying, "My daughter has no brother to defend her, but she has me, and I want to say to you that if these stories ever appear again I will leave the White House and thrash the man who dares utter them."[3]

- Herbert Hoover required reporters to submit their questions ahead of time and in writing. He chided them, "The President of the United States will not be questioned like a chicken thief by men whose names he does not even know."[4]

- Franklin D. Roosevelt signed a picture of himself that was then hung for journalists in the White House Press Room. His inscription read simply, "From their victim."[5]

- Richard Nixon had a lot of things to say to—and about—the press. Among his more biting comments was this remark he made to journalists in a 1973 news conference: "Don't get the impression that you arouse my anger...You see, one can only be angry with those he respects."[6]

PRESIDENTS MEET THE PRESS

Access to the president of the United States is tightly regulated by White House aides, and even regular members of the White House press corps don't have that much of a chance to interact one-on-one with the commander-in-chief. That is why the presidential news conference is so important. On these occasions, a roomful of reporters is brought into contact with the president and ostensibly can ask him whatever they wish. In reality, even that access is not equal among the assembled reporters, as written and unwritten rules of conduct apply. Each president who has employed the news conference treats it differently, sometimes a little and sometimes a lot.

The press conference is an important part of any presidency, but it is not the only way the president communicates with journalists or with the public as a whole. The following are some of the ways presidents have used to communicate either with journalists or directly to the public.

1. Formal messages, such as the State of the Union address each year.
2. Special messages to Congress or individual legislators.
3. Prime-time television addresses made by the president to the American people, live from the Oval Office.
4. Daily White House briefings held by the president's press secretary.
5. Presidential proclamations.

6. White House announcements or statements such as the one Truman made that ordered the Atomic Energy Commission to proceed with work on the hydrogen bomb.

7. Presidential speeches made at selected, appropriate venues around the country.

8. Issuance of Executive Orders.

9. Weekly radio addresses, which President Reagan used so effectively.

10. "Fireside chats" that Franklin Roosevelt conducted on a regular basis with the American public.

11. Intentional White House "leaks" to the press, sometimes used to float trial balloons to obtain public or Congressional reaction before a decision is actually made.

12. Background briefings held by presidential staff for members of the press.

The highest-profile event, however, is the president's news conference. Presidential historian Joseph Spear lists several advantages of these press conferences, including the following:[7]

- The conference affords a fairly direct way for the president to announce executive action or policy, and to explain his viewpoint on issues.

- It makes possible, for domestic or worldwide consumption, a democratic exchange between the chief executive and the press...on matters of interest and importance to the public.

- It multiplies the possibilities of the White House as a sounding board for altering, making, and shaping public opinion.

- In its limited way, subject always to the willingness of the president to respond, it is an American equivalent of the British device for questioning the government on matters of policy.

- However it may vary from time to time or from administration to administration, its cumulative effect is to make the executive more responsible and more responsive to the public.

On the negative side, of course, is the fact that each president treats the press conference with different degrees of importance, some holding many, some holding few of them. Also, journalists are not very effective, at times, in getting direct and specific answers from the president who has the freedom to respond in any way he sees fit, even if it's a response that does not fit the question. In sum, the president's news conference is his to control, and he can choose when to hold it, which reporters to acknowledge, which questions to answer and which to dodge, and he can end it when he pleases.

FROM WILSON TO BUSH

The presidential news conference was not begun until the administration of Woodrow Wilson early in the twentieth century. Before that, presidents had no formal system for interacting with journalists. Even though Wilson originated the press conference, he didn't use it very long, because he became angered with journalists for prying into his family's affairs and because he spent more and more of his time and energy on the approaching war in Europe and later in Mexico. So it wasn't long before the newfound press conference was shelved by the Wilson presidency. It was renewed under Warren G. Harding and has remained a permanent fixture in the White House ever since. Harding had been a newspaper editor and publisher, and he understood the importance of keeping journalists informed. His presidency lasted only 29 months until his death, however, and it was up to his successor, Calvin Coolidge, to continue it.

President Coolidge is believed by some to have held more news conferences than any other president, historian James Pollard notes.[8] Others disagree, noting that some of these events did not live up to the nature of an actual press conference. It was left to Franklin Delano Roosevelt to add new luster to the presidential news conference and to give it a status unseen before. During his three-term, 12 years in office, FDR held just shy of 1,000 news conferences, averaging about two each week. That is a record unmatched by any president since. Roosevelt's staff laid down rules concerning background and off-the-record comments, and he delivered commentary on the events with the understanding that this "editorializing" would not be attributed to him in print. In many ways, the White House news conference reached its zenith under FDR. Pollard notes, "It would be difficult to calculate the total effect of his news conferences in terms of the political information they yielded, their play upon the forces of public opinion, or their contribution to the shaping of national and international policy; but the net effect would certainly be considerable."[9]

Harry Truman also used the presidential press conference to good advantage, and generally provided a lot of information to the public through them. In all, Truman conducted 324 news conferences, an average of three to four a month for his nearly eight years in office. Truman, like FDR, was on familiar terms with reporters, and also like FDR, he often delivered his comments in homespun fashion. Nevertheless, on a professional level, Truman and the press remained adversaries, as have all presidents in their relationships with the media. Still, in his press conferences he often was candid, sometimes catching reporters off-guard with his homespun honesty which somehow didn't seem to fit the world of Washington policies or the larger Cold War. As the press conferences became more publicized and important with regard to Cold War strategy, some of that candor gave way to careful scripting by the president. One development that affected the latter Truman press conferences was the emergence of television news. While his press conferences were not carried live on TV, nevertheless the addition of the visual medium added weight to the news conferences and to the impact of what was said when the footage was carried later on the networks.

Dwight Eisenhower carried on the tradition of press conferences, although he seemed more fatherly and stiff than were his two predecessors in the White House. It wasn't that Eisenhower was unused to dealing with journalists; indeed, he had spent several years working with the press while serving as

Supreme Commander of Allied Forces in Europe during World War II. Still, under Ike, the number of press conferences dropped significantly, and he held only fourteen during his first eight months in office. On several occasions he became annoyed with the questioning and actually lost his composure at times.

When John F. Kennedy entered the White House, he brought renewed enthusiasm to the presidential news conference. In his forties, he was still young, and he liked to crack jokes with reporters and appear generally in good spirits. He was briefed well before the news conferences and usually had quick and on-target responses, often with a twist of humor thrown in. Like a few other presidents—such as Harding—Kennedy had worked as a journalist himself, albeit briefly, before entering politics. It gave him insight into the daily job of journalism and an understanding, if not appreciation, of the challenges journalists were up against and why they asked questions as they did sometimes. Kennedy developed friendships with several members of the White House press corps, and those relationships proved beneficial when it came to the image many journalists portrayed of him and his presidency.

When Kennedy was assassinated in November 1963, Vice-President Lyndon B. Johnson lurched into action as the nation's chief executive. If the press was worried about this salty Texan separating himself from members of the news media, many of those fears were allayed during the first few months of LBJ's presidency. His press conferences were much more frequent and impulsive than were Kennedy's (he held some 26 in his first six months of office), and they were much more informal than under Kennedy. LBJ seemed to draw up some of the homespun humor of Harry Truman in speaking to journalists, and many appreciated it. He could also be barbed, however, if he felt wronged by the press. Like Kennedy, Johnson conferred individually with journalists and had many friends in the press corps. Even as the years in the White House—and the pressure that the prolonged Vietnam War brought—dragged on, Johnson continued his tradition of frequent press conferences down to the end of his first—and last—full term when he chose not to run for re-election.

The presidency of Richard M. Nixon brought noticeable changes in the relationship between the White House and the press. Nixon had a general disdain for journalists that, at times, reached the point of outright paranoia. Several journalists wound up on Nixon's infamous "enemies list," and he often regarded the press as his enemy. He had felt he was treated badly by the press in his ill-fated earlier run for the White House in 1962, and he is often remembered for his famous admonition to journalists, "For sixteen years, ever since the Hiss case, you've had a lot of—a lot of fun...Just think how much you're going to be missing. You won't have Nixon to kick around anymore, because, gentlemen, this is my last press conference..."[10] In the dawning of the age of live television, President Nixon had anything but a television persona; many believe it is what cost him the 1962 campaign against John F. Kennedy. He appeared awkward in front of the camera and would sometimes show sweat as he took questions from reporters. He held fewer press conferences than his predecessors, and he struggled through many of them. The relationship between Nixon and the press went from bad to worse when the cover-up of Watergate began unraveling in the face of intense investigative work by the *Washington Post* and *New York Times*. In time, Nixon sealed himself off from most members of the press and his West Wing became a kind of fortress. In cutting himself off from the press (seeing his ability to control it as a failing effort), the case could be made that President Nixon also cut himself off from external sources of information. He relied totally on what his closest aides and friends would tell him, and often he was told what these people felt he wanted to hear. CBS's Bob Schieffer, who succeeded Dan Rather as White House correspondent, said that what Nixon did, in effect, was to cut himself off from reality.[11]

The short presidency of Gerald Ford was a breath of fresh air to many reporters, but was relatively unremarkable in terms of breaking new ground with the news media via press conferences. The one memorable event that did occur under Ford was the resignation of his press secretary, Jerald terHorst, who said he could no longer continue to serve after President Ford pardoned Richard Nixon, an act he could not personally support. Overall, the White House press reported liking President Ford a lot. He was very much the kind of man they could understand: affable, competent, and—as a former football player at the University of Michigan—a man in love with football. He seemed at ease with members of the press, which again was very different from his predecessor who considered journalists enemies. Since Ford was completing the term left by the resigning Nixon, much of his own term was taken up with campaigning for what would have been his first full term as president. That was an opportunity that was never realized because of a relative unknown from the State of Georgia: Jimmy Carter.

Jimmy Carter and his southern cadre of aides breezed into the White House next, and again returned a folksiness—although a more distanced one—to the news conference and to his relationship with the press. Jody Powell was his press secretary, and was one who was generally respected by the White House press corps. Carter, with his ubiquitous grin and southern drawl, often gave one-on-one interviews with high-profile journalists in addition to holding regular press conferences. Many journalists, however, reported that Carter's grin belied a temper that often was directed at his own staff as well as individual journalists. His blunt manner was a turnoff to many in the press.[12] Bob Schieffer described often unseen the relationship between Carter and the press this way:

> Many of the reporters who covered him during the campaign were turned off by his blunt manner. They believed Carter tolerated them as people who had to be dealt with in order to be elected, but few thought he had any feeling for hem, one way or the other. Sam Donaldson of ABC, who had covered Carter longer than any other reporter that year, remembered how, late one Friday evening in Keene, New Hampshire, Carter had canceled a plane that had been chartered to take him

and a small group of reporters to Boston. Carter was furious that the plane was late, and decided to drive. Donaldson couldn't blame him, but when he asked, "Do you have an extra seat, Governor?" Carter said one word, "No," and walked away, leaving his staffers and the reporters stranded. Donaldson finally found a rental car and gave Carter's staffers a ride back to Boston.[13]

Other reporters, such as Schieffer himself, reported getting along well with President Carter, as the president would sometimes chat privately with him, once or twice at a diner in Plains. Carter's down-home style, which proved to be at odds with formal Washington, D.C., was also shown in the demeanor and practice of his staff, including his press secretary. Carter chose Jody Powell for that job, a man who at 32 had spent a lot of time with him as his driver who worked his way up in the president-elect's staff. Schieffer said that Powell lived in the same Georgia motel where the press stayed in the fall prior to Carter's entrance to the White House. "When Powell had an announcement, he would signal us by hanging a bedsheet on the balcony railing outside his room...But Powell was a true advisor to Carter, and because he knew Carter so well and was usually part of the decision-making process, we knew that what he told us reflected the president's thinking. I don't know of a press secretary since who has had the access Powell had," Schieffer recalled.[14]

As his first and only term in the White House wore on and pressures mounted, however, his tone became more serious and his press conferences somewhat fewer in number. The end for Carter came during the American hostage crisis in Iran and with an economy that grew depressing for the American voters. Many believe Carter has done more good for the country after the White House than any previous former president. Through his initiatives with the Carter Center in Atlanta, Carter gives many interviews to journalists and often enlists the press in helping bring attention to needed issues and programs around the world.

In large measure, the presidency of Ronald Reagan was one of the most popular America has seen since the days of Roosevelt or Truman. This professional actor/turned politician had the charisma to turn voters on, and he continued to use it once elected to the White House. His relationship with the press, however, was often stage-managed, much as his life in motion pictures had been. Earlier in this book we took a look at how his chief media aide, Michael Deaver, positioned the president to the best advantage with the media and controlled access to the president in a very tight and purposeful manner. As has been mentioned, Deaver believed in the power of the visual overcoming the spoken word on television, and he often positioned his boss in the best possible visual frame to project a positive image that often countered the negative story that was being told by the on-air reporter. Reagan continued the tradition of the presidential news conference, but he also would go directly to the American people via prime-time talks from the Oval Office, and by way of his popular weekly radio address. The Reagan presidency wound up with an hour-long interview by

President and Nancy Reagan granted to Mike Wallace on CBS's popular *60 Minutes*. The questions were far-reaching, and Wallace pulled no punches especially with his questions to Mrs. Reagan, who had achieved some controversy in her role as the "power behind the throne."

When George Herbert Walker Bush assumed the mantle of presidency following Reagan, he walked into a media storm created in part by controversy surrounding his role in what was known as "Irangate." The issue was, how much did Bush know about the deal to trade arms to the Iranians for the lives of American hostages who were freed when Ronald Reagan entered the White House? The arms-for-hostages story was late in breaking and Bush, as former head of the CIA and vice-president under Reagan, was believed by many to have been a part of the arms deal or at least to have known about it. These were charges he vehemently denied, and that denial reached its zenith during a famous 1988 interview with Dan Rather, anchor of CBS Evening News. In that interview, done during the heat of Bush's campaign, Rather broached the subject of what Bush knew of the arms-for-hostages plan, and when he knew it. Rather zeroed in on a meeting at which others said Bush was present; it was a meeting in which the arms-for-hostages deal was discussed, and Secretary of State George Schultz was also there. The infamous portion of that January 25, 1998, televised interview went this way:[15]

RATHER:
You weren't in the meeting?

BUSH:
I'm not suggesting. I'm just saying I don't remember it.

RATHER:
I don't want to be argumentative, Mr. Vice President.

BUSH:
You do, Dan.

RATHER:
No...no, sir, I don't.

BUSH:
This is not a great night, because I want to talk about why I want to be president, why those 41 percent of the people are supporting me. And I don't think it's fair...

RATHER:
And Mr. Vice President, if these questions are—

BUSH:
...to judge my whole career by a rehash on Iran. How would you like it if I judged your career by those seven minutes when you walked off the set in New York? [Note: In reality, Rather was in Miami and he was off the set for

six minutes, when CBS let the NFL game of the week run into the time slot reserved for Rather's newscast.]

RATHER:
Well, Mister. . .

BUSH:
. . .Would you like that?

RATHER:
Mr. Vice President. . .

BUSH:
I have respect for you, but I don't have respect for what you're doing here tonight.

RATHER:
Mr. Vice President, I think you'll agree that your qualification for President and what kind of leadership you'd bring to the country, what kind of government you'd have, what kind of people you have around you. . .

BUSH:
Exactly.

RATHER:
. . .is much more important that what you just referred to. I'd be happy to. . .

BUSH:
Well, I want to be judged on the whole record, and you're not giving an opportunity.

RATHER:
And I'm trying to set the record straight, Mr. Vice President.

BUSH:
You invited me to come here and talk about—I thought—the whole record.

RATHER:
I want you to talk about the record. You sat in a meeting with George Shultz. . .

BUSH:
Yes, and I've given you an answer.

RATHER:
He got apoplectic when he found out that you were. . .

BUSH:
He didn't get apoplectic. You have to ask Don Regan. Ask. . .

RATHER:
. . .you and the President were being party to sending missiles to the Ayatollah. . .

BUSH:
Ask...

RATHER:
...the Ayatollah of Iran. Can you explain how—you were supposed to be the—you are—you're an anti terrorist expert. We—Iran was officially a terrorist state.

BUSH:
I've already explained that, Dan.

RATHER:
You went around telling—you—you...

BUSH:
I wanted those hostages—I wanted Mr. Buckley out of there...

RATHER:
Mr. Vice President, the question is—but you—made us hypocrites in the face of the world.

BUSH:
Before he was killed, which he has been killed.

RATHER:
How could you...

BUSH:
That was bad.

RATHER:
...sign on to such a policy?! And the question is...

BUSH:
Well, I had the same reason the President signed on to it.

RATHER:
...what does that tell us about your record?

BUSH:
The same reason the President signed on to it. When a CIA agent is being tortured to death, maybe you err on the side of a human life. But everybody's admitted mistakes. I've admitted mistakes. And you want to dwell on them, and I want to talk about the values we believe in and experience and the integrity that goes with all of this, and what's—I'm going to do about education, and you're... there's nothing new here. I thought this was a news program. What is new?

RATHER:
Well, I had hoped, Mr. Vice President, that you would tell us to whom you expressed your reservations...

A media firestorm ensued over this interview, and the next night it was Dan Rather who was the focus of it as other network reporters tried to interview him on whether he thought he went too far in trying to get the vice president to address the issue of Iran-Contra. Rather responded that he was not the story; that the story was still what Bush knew about the arms deal, when he knew it, and whether he was being forthright about it to the American people.

In modern times, President Reagan was rivaled as a communicator only by President Bill Clinton. A key difference between the two presidents and their relationship to the press, however, was that Reagan was so enormously popular with the American people, while the public had differing views about Clinton. In general, much of the voting population seemed to like Clinton in his official role as president, but they had mixed feelings about the way he conducted his personal life. The point—as some network correspondents such as CBS's Leslie Stahl have made—is that Reagan was so popular with the public that it was sometimes hard to get her news executives to agree to negative stories about him. They did not want to run the risk of alienating the American public unless absolutely necessary.[16] And, Stahl added, she was sometimes asked to "wallpaper" those negative stories with "pretty pictures" to lessen the harmful effect on Reagan. Apparently, journalists were not under any such constrictions when it came to reporting on Clinton. They jumped on him early during his 1992 presidential campaign over the Gennifer Flowers affair, and hammered him during his later escapades, most notably the Monica Lewinsky incident, which brought him to the point of impeachment.

Clinton held his share of press conferences, and he often spoke to gatherings of journalists, including the national convention of the American Society of Newspaper Editors, held in Washington, D.C. At one of these conventions, Clinton did what he did best: spoke for about twenty minutes and spent most of the next hour working his way through a sea of outstretched journalists' hands, looking editors in the eye at close range and making each feel they were the only one in the huge, crowded ballroom of the Marriott Hotel. Much like President Carter, Clinton sported a ubiquitous grin that often belied other feelings, especially toward the press. Clinton came into the White House with a lot of frustration over the press that had hounded him about his personal life and his avoidance of the military draft during the Vietnam War. And he appointed a press secretary in Dee Dee Myers who really had no journalistic credentials, and who had a rough time dealing with the press. But part of that trouble was because Clinton had another spokesman in George Stephanopoulos, who actually received the physical office space normally reserved for the press secretary. Stephanopoulos gave the afternoon newsmaking briefings, while Myers gave the morning briefings. It seemed to many that Myers, a 31 year old woman with no reporting experience, was handed the job by a president wanting credit for naming the first woman to the press secretary's position.[17] Because she was not given the access to Clinton that Stephanopoulos had, and because she had no journalistic experience, the press found her likeable but not very helpful.

On January 5, 1995, she was replaced by Mike McCurry, who moved as spokesman for the State Department to spokesman for the president. McCurry seemed better suited to the job, and he was soon being ranked by journalists as among the best of presidential secretaries of all time.[18] Among his initiatives were off-the-record sessions with White House correspondents. Part of his purpose for these sessions was to obtain their perspectives on how to improve the working relationship between the White House and the press. As Nelson said, "He instructed his staff to deal courteously with reporters and return their telephone calls. 'The overall atmosphere became much kinder and gentler,' said one correspondent."[19]

When George W. Bush entered the White House in 2000, he of course did so on the basis of a turbulent election which was thrust into the U.S. Supreme Court for a decision following the balloting debacle in the deciding state of Florida. Bush was given the Electoral College advantage over Democratic Challenger Al Gore, but he had lost the popular vote. As such, he led with no popular mandate like other presidents had. There was speculation – both in the press and on television programs like Saturday Night Live and the David Letterman Show, that he would be overshadowed by his more experienced vice president, Dick Cheney, who had served his father so loyally when the senior Bush was president. This younger Bush was skewered in skit after skit on Saturday Night Live, usually in the framework of a president who had a smaller playschool desk overshadowed by the larger, adult desk of Cheney. In his relations with the press, Bush's reviews were mixed early on. Many journalists reported him affable and joking, both one-on-one and on the campaign trail. Once in the White House, however, journalists' access to Bush became much more difficult.

SUMMARY

Every president treats the press somewhat differently, and each president has a variety of ways of communicating with the news media and with the public at large. One of the key methods all presidents use is the press conference, although more recently, presidents have been circumventing the media in going directly to the American people through live televised speeches and through the Internet. The relationship between the press and presidents is one of mutual need, just as it is for the media and other politicians. Presidents need to curry the favor of the nation's press, while the media obviously need the president as the nation's chief newsmaker. Every president since George Washington must have, at times, wished the democratic system could work without the prying eyes of the press, or at least wished that journalists would look elsewhere than the White House for their daily fix of news.

CHAPTER 9

Conducting War in a Media Age

Nowhere is the news media's impact more important than in its coverage of war. Journalists are the eyes and ears of viewers and readers when it comes to war and rumors of wars. To a democratic government waging war, the news media (as well as entertainment media) become a two-edged sword influencing their ability to wage the war. On the one hand, government and military officials may need the media to help promote their vision of why the war is necessary and why the country should fight to win. On the other hand, the media can become a potential obstacle in waging the war with the graphic stories, photos, and video they show to the American people of American soldiers fighting and dying in battle. Journalists become a further impediment when they devote coverage to debates surrounding how well the war is being waged, and whether the war is even necessary. The truism is—and always has been—that it is difficult for the American government to sustain a long war in the face of intense media scrutiny. It is this coverage which (as time passes) looks more at the gray areas for fighting the war than at the black and white polarity the government would like its people to see. Throughout history, when the bullets start flying, no American presidential administration has wanted its media to debate the gray areas of the war. To government leaders, this is the time to take sides, and they point out clearly and repeatedly the good/evil dichotomy of the two sides (and there are just two, according to government framing) at war. A historical look at American warfare in the twentieth and twenty-first centuries shows how this dilemma is reflected in war after war this country has fought.

WORLD WAR I

The so-called "Great War" started in Europe in August of 1914, morphing into a worldwide war by 1917. America's entry into it under the Wilson Administration (elected under the banner of "he kept us out of war"), was supposed to make the world "safe for democracy." The great European dynasties had toppled, and the peace that Western Europe had enjoyed since the early 1870s was over. The spark that ignited the war in 1914 was the so-called "Balkan incident" as the German Army marched into Brussels. An American correspondent was there to record the incident, and Richard Harding Davis's account became part of great American journalistic lore as he spoke of "...one unbroken steel-gray column...24 hours later is still coming...not men marching but a force of nature like a tidal wave..."[1].

These were pre-television days, even pre-radio days, and it took a while for descriptions like that to flash back to most Americans. But when they did, the images and the seriousness of the events hit with a thud, and many Americans knew there was trouble in Europe...and maybe for the United States up ahead. American denial about the events in Europe would become harder to sustain in the months and years ahead. America opposed one-nation domination of Europe, and not just for reasons of morality. There were economic concerns involved as well. America was realizing that it needed to be a major player in the global economy, and the success of America depended to a large extent on the success of capitalism in Europe. That seemed threatened by having Germany dominate Europe, its people, and its economy. In fact, despite a press that became overwhelmingly supportive of the American entry into the war after 1917, there were still many holdouts who had alternative views that America was in it just because of the threat to its wallets. Of course that alternative view is often present when Americans think about wars which involve them, right down to the second Gulf War where the mantra, "it's all about oil," has been heard from many dissidents.

Additionally, America had given rise to an unprecedented number of international peace movements. Many new peace organizations were formed in the first fifteen years of the twentieth century. They included the Carnegie Endowment for International Peace (formed in 1910), and the Church Peace Union (1914). Also, while the mainstream American sentiment seemed to lie with English-speaking people of Western Europe, there were ethnic groups in America—key among them the Irish—who had great mistrust of the British for other reasons. Geographically, the American Midwest seemed more isolationist than did those on the East Coast. After all, America was seen as a country protected by two oceans with more than enough issues and problems of its own. Why should they join in a European war?

A war often takes a spark to get it going, and World War I was no exception. In this case, though, there was a series of sparks. One came as early as 1915 when the luxury liner the Lusitania was sunk off the Irish coast, with nearly 1,200 souls perishing, including 114 Americans. The culprit was a German submarine. The sinking spelled trouble for Wilson's plan to somehow arbitrate the European dispute, and more trouble ensued when Germany stepped up its unrestricted submarine warfare program in February of 1917. This resulted in a break of diplomatic relations between America and Germany. The final spark came with the Allied interception of a note dated January 16, 1917, from German Foreign Minister Arthur Zimmermann to the Mexican government. In it, Zimmermann offered the return of New Mexico, Arizona, and Texas to Mexico if they would join Germany in helping to defeat America in war. Agents for British intelligence, who had intercepted the infamous note, made sure it found its way to President Wilson, who released it two months later to the media. The note did its job in helping to galvanize more support for American entry into the European war.

America declared war on April 6, 1917, over the objections of some influential newspapers including the *Chicago Tribune, Washington Post, Los Angeles Times, San Francisco Chronicle* and *Cleveland Plain Dealer.* These newspapers still preached isolationism and anti-interventionism, and warned of the dangers of becoming involved in someone else's war. But their voices were drowned out by most other newspapers in the country, as Americans felt they saw the handwriting on the wall in the dangers of German domination of Europe.

To help cement this resolve, the Wilson Administration created the Committee on Public Information (CPI) just one week after the war declaration. Brought in to chair the committee was a respected newsman in George Creel. Before he was through, he eventually mobilized some 150,000 Americans to help him carry out the wide-ranging mission of the CPI, which included disseminating facts about the war effort and to coordinate the American government's propaganda efforts. As Emery notes of Creel's efforts:

> The opportunity Wilson gave to Creel was a greater one than any other person had enjoyed in the propaganda arena...Creel first opened up government news channels to the Washington correspondents and insisted that only news of troop movements, ship sailings, and other events of strictly military character should be withheld. He issued a brief explanatory code calling on the newspapers to censor such news themselves, voluntarily. Throughout the war, newspaper editors generally went beyond Creel's minimum requests in their desire to aid the war effort. In May 1917 the CPI began publishing an Official bulletin in which releases were reprinted in newspaper form. Before the war was over this publication reached a daily circulation of 118,000.[2]

By any account, Creel's committee was successful in aiding the war effort and uniting public opinion. In fact, writing about it in his classic book *Public Opinion,* journalist Walter Lippmann called it the single greatest example of creating one unified public opinion ever achieved.[3] Not only did the CPI serve well as a propaganda tool, it is also remarkable that most of its 6,000 press releases were deemed accurate by the journalists using them, and few were called into question, according to researcher Walton E. Bean, who wrote in 1941: "It may be doubted that the CPI's record for honesty will ever be equaled in the official war news of a major power."[4] Emery notes, however, this assessment doesn't take into account sins of omission or concealment by the government of facts relating to the war.[5]

To a large degree, World War I was characterized by a press that did not need reminding of its patriotic duty by the American government, because most journalists evidenced that spirit voluntarily, offering to censor their own reports beyond the official censorship guidelines. To help insure that dissident (mostly socialist and German-language) papers didn't go too far astray, however, Congress passed the Espionage Act of June 15, 1917, and the Sedition Act of 1918, to insure journalists didn't impede the war effort by their overly critical commentary. The Espionage Act banned offending papers from the U.S. mail (which was how most were delivered), and the Sedition Act made it a crime to write or publish "any disloyal, profane, scurrilous or abusive language about the form of government of the Unites States or the Constitution, military or naval forces, flag, or the uniform...or to use language intended to bring these ideas and institutions into contempt, scorn, contumely, or disrepute." Mainstream newspapers—including the newspapers of William Randolph Hearst, which opposed the war—remained unaffected by these laws, the brunt of which fell more heavily on socialist publications.

In terms of battlefield coverage, American correspondents distinguished themselves in World War I and found themselves free to roam where they pleased and report without military escorts (at least in General John Pershing's area). Everything the correspondents wrote, however, had to be filtered through the censors of the Military Intelligence Service. Reports dealing with specific battles, dead and wounded, and troop identifications were released only if they had been mentioned in official communiqués. In all, some 500 American reporters were in Europe as America entered the war, and that number grew once Americans actually took to the battlefields. One invention of World War I was the kind of "soldier's journalism" that would come to characterize World War II: the view of the war from the average soldier or sailor. This news was typified in the eight-page newspaper called *Stars and Stripes*, which first appeared in Paris in 1918. It is still published today.

World War I ended with the signing of the Treaty of Versailles in June 1919, and Wilson had hopes it would result in—among other things—the establishment of a League of Nations, which America would join. Congress refused to ratify America's entry into that league, however, as the spirit of internationalism faded at war's end.

WORLD WAR II

With Germany still reeling from the humiliation of World War I and the price that the war—as well as the peace—cost them, the country was buoyed by the rhetoric and promises of Adolph Hitler as he rose to power during the early

1930s. To the outside world—especially with 20/20 hindsight—what looks like a madman was seen by many Germans as the man with a plan to make Germany feel proud of itself once again. However, in August 1939 when Germany and Russia signed a neutrality agreement allowing the German army freedom to march into Poland without fear of Russian retaliation, the rest of the world took notice. Russia was to get eastern Poland out of the deal, and the German aggression was on. The next month both the British and French were forced to declare war against the aggressor as he turned his sights on them. Theirs were defensive actions, however, devoid of any offensive front into Germany or neighboring countries. President Franklin Delano Roosevelt responded to the German aggression by quickly upping his efforts to aid the British and French in their struggle. Congress repealed the Neutrality Act which had cast the United States as an isolationist power since the close of World War I, and sentiment began running strong in the United States for England and France. Not all newspapers fell in line, however, and one of the largest dissenters was the *Chicago Tribune*, which had opposed the U.S. entry into World War I.

There were only a handful of American correspondents in Europe when Germany began its march into neighboring countries, and one of them was William L. Shirer, a reporter who would later distinguish himself by writing *The Rise and Fall of the Third Reich*. Before Germany's march into Poland, Shirer was filing stories for CBS Radio, outlining what appeared to be a kind of ethnic cleansing crusade by the Third Reich, targeted at Jewish persons. He wrote about the abusive treatment the Jews received in Germany and the rumors of greater atrocities, but he said later that he got the feeling Americans didn't want to hear that news, nor did they want to hear much about Germany at all. He reasoned that Americans were happy, as they emerged from the Depression years, that they had moved past discussions of World War I, and wanted to hear more about the sports heroes and celebrities of the day. Actually, he noted in an article for The Boston Globe, he felt many Americans (including some newspaper publishers) felt Hitler should try his hand at rebuilding Germany, especially if it meant that country could stop Russia's growing Communist designs on the world.[6] He said he and other reporters would send back their stories about German atrocities, only to find them shoved to the back of the newspaper or the bottom of the broadcast, if they were used at all.

When the German army began to move, however, much of this American denial began to change as the spring of 1940 brought unmistakable signs of Hitler's intention to dominate Europe. That was the season of Germany's invasions of Denmark and Norway, followed by a huge strike against France, Belgium, and Holland. The fears that had propelled America into World War I were back again. The debates grew between the isolationists and interventionists in the United States, and each had its leaders. The isolationists championed Col. Charles A. Lindbergh's endorsement of the America First Committee, while Kansas newspaper editor William Allen White headed the Committee to Defend America by Aiding the Allies. President Roosevelt called America to action to become "the great arsenal of democracy," and warned that a British defeat would mean German domination of Europe as well as Asia, Australia, Africa, and the seas. America's actual entrance into the war was preceded by the Lend-Lease Act of 1941, authorizing the president to provide massive aid to the Allies in Europe as they struggled against the German-led Axis powers. He was putting in place a program to unify Americans for entering the war on the Allies side when the Japanese attacked the American Naval fleet at Pearl Harbor on December 7, 1941. The unprovoked surprise attack on an early Sunday morning shocked Americans and dealt a crippling blow to the U.S. Navy. Roosevelt responded to Congress the next day with a request for a declaration of war against Japan. Three days later Germany declared war against the United States.

As the war began, the Espionage Act was still on the books from World War I, as was the Trading With the Enemy Act, which gave the government the right to inspect communiqués coming in and going out of the United States. Most of the Sedition Act's provisions had been repealed by this time. Again, German-language and socialist newspapers were the targets of the Espionage Act, and few mainstream publications were hit with sanctions. In place of the old Committee on Public Information (CPI), Roosevelt established two separated offices, both led by experienced newsmen. The Office of Censorship was headed by Byron Price, who was executive editor of the Associated Press and—like Creel in World War I—respected by his peers. That office issued a Code of Wartime Practices for the American Press in January 1942, outlining the kinds of stories that could be released for publication and those which should be withheld until officially released. This became an important handbook for American correspondents who, like their predecessors in World War I, required little urging to follow the rules and protect American troops and the U.S. war effort. And, also like their World War I counterparts, when American correspondents in World War II faced ambiguous situations in the field, they often erred on the side of censorship rather than taking a chance of revealing important secrets.

The second office Roosevelt established was the Office of War Information (OWI), headed by Elmer Davis, formerly of CBS Radio and the New York Times. Like the CPI in World War I, this office functioned mainly to provide Americans news about the war effort. World War II produced a generally cooperative effort by the news media, which even provided free advertising space for war-related ads.

Actual military censorship in the field varied, depending on which branch of service a correspondent was reporting on, or which commander was in charge of that theatre of the war. Many reporters felt the British Admiralty and the U.S. Navy were most stringent about withholding details, although General Douglas MacArthur was criticized for his heavyhanded censorship in the Pacific. In Europe, however, General Dwight D. Eisenhower was usually given good marks by correspondents. One problem military commanders and their field censors had in World War II that they had not had in World War I was the radio broadcast. Obviously, radio could reach people faster than newspapers, and commanders had to learn how to deal with this new medium and its many correspondents in the war.

Coverage of the war was deemed the most comprehensive and accurate the world had seen up to that point. More than 1,600 correspondents—both newspaper and radio—were accredited during the war's duration, and some 500 correspondents were in the field at any one time. As media technology increased to the point of developing mobile broadcast units and tape recordings, correspondents could report from virtually anywhere, such as CBS's Edward R. Murrow did when he reported from an American bomber as it flew one of its missions. Perhaps the best known and most beloved correspondents of the war was Ernie Pyle from Indiana, who wrote a from-the-foxhole style of GI journalism. His fame grew during the war, and today the Indiana University Journalism School is named for him. Pyle survived many battles in Europe, only to move on to the Pacific when the war in Europe ended and be struck down by a Japanese sniper's bullet during the Okinawa campaign. Pyle was one of 37 American correspondents who lost their lives in World War II fighting.

World War II was covered not only with words in newspapers and over the radio, but also with some terrifically revealing news photography. Photojournalism was an important part of the war's coverage, and the venues for those photos ranged far and wide from the photo-oriented *Life* and *Look* magazines to daily papers and small-town weeklies across America. This was probably the war that the world realized how important visual imagery is in conveying the horrors of war and in transporting readers to the bloody scenes of battle. But photojournalists also caught some singular moments which bespoke victory as a result of self-sacrifice of American troops. Probably the best-known single image from World War II was the photo by Joe Rosenthal of the Associated Press, picturing a handful of Marines and sailors planting the American flag on Mount Suribachi in the battle for the island of Iwo Jima. Like other memorable photos, such as one of Babe Ruth acknowledging the throngs of fans in his last game at Yankee Stadium, it was not a shot the photographer was originally pleased with. In both of these memorable photos, the actual faces of the subjects are obscured (Ruth was shot from behind as he waved to the crowd), but the images more than did their job. The photo of the flag-raising at Iwo Jima inspired Americans and made them even more grateful for the job their troops were doing overseas. As for the government, they saw in this single photo a chance to raise more funds through the sale of war bonds; enough money that might enable the country to bring a speedier end to the war in the Pacific. The two surviving Marines and one sailor from that photo were quickly taken out of action, returned to the states, and were used by the government as poster boys for a final big push in war bond sales. Their story was told in a 2006 film by Clint Eastwood called *Flags of Our Fathers*.

In 1945, the American press had two major stories to deal with. One was the final stages of the War in Europe and the fighting in the Pacific; the other was the death of America's longest-serving president. Franklin Roosevelt died of a massive brain hemorrhage at 63 in April 1945, while serving an unprecedented fourth term. The news startled the world, and Harry S Truman was sworn in as president within a few hours of Roosevelt's death. Now it would fall to a new president to determine how best to bring an end to the war in the Pacific and, ultimately, Truman of course decided to use the atomic bomb, which had been under secret development for some time. It was a controversial decision at the time, and remains one today.

VIETNAM

The trend toward American involvement in foreign conflicts that didn't seem as much of a direct threat as World War II had actually began before Vietnam with the Korean Conflict. In fact, it was the first American "war" to be labeled a "conflict." As Truman sent troops to Korea to stop the designs of North Korea from moving into South Korea, the rationale for the war remained a mystery to some Americans, especially as it dragged on from 1950–53. Gone was the strict public unity behind the World War II effort, and in its place came an America divided over the role of the United States. in Korea. The debate was played out in the news media as peace negotiators in Panmunjom moved toward a truce in 1953 that brought an end to the fighting but not a final resolution to the North/South Korean conflict.

Following the Korean War, Americans enjoyed a decade of peace, free from involvement in wars or conflicts. All that ended, however, in the Southeast Asian nation known as Vietnam. Here is how one team of writers described America's involvement in that war and the role the press played:

> The American phase of the 30-year struggle in Indochina—in Vietnam, in Cambodia, and in Laos—became perhaps the most thoroughly covered war in history. Certainly it caused more moral searching than ever, and by the time the United States withdrew in 1975, it seemed that it represented a revulsion against the Cold War mentality and an ebbing of the spirit of "Manifest Destiny." Much credit should accrue to the print and broadcast correspondents and photographers covering the war, including the more than 50 who died, as well as those few who clarified the issues through their dissent at home.[7]

The story of how Vietnam came to engulf American troops for more than a decade is beyond the purpose of this chapter. Suffice it to say that, following the surrender of the Japanese in World War II, Vietnam was proclaimed a Democratic Republic by its leader Ho Chi Minh. The next year, the French returned to the capital of Saigon and began fighting Ho Chi Minh's forces. The French put in emperor Bao Dai as chief of state in 1948, and that regime received financial support from the U.S. government in 1950. Eager to keep the country out of Communist hands, the American government was responsible for the lion's share of the cost of the fighting there, but the French were ultimately defeated by the Viet Minh forces at a place called Dienbienphu. The resulting treaty divided Vietnam at the seventeenth parallel, and was supposed to result in reunification by way of national elections two years later. However, all did not go according to plan, as the Bao Dai regime refused to sign the pact. So the American government created the Southeast Asia Treaty Organization (SEATO), and vowed to protect Vietnam from Communist aggression. Bao Dai was ousted by Premier Ngo Dinh Diem, who would not allow the national elections to take place and—with the help of U.S. military advisors—started equipping and training his armed forces starting in 1955. Those Vietnamese opposing Diem and his regime in South Vietnam created the National Liberation Front. Its armed guerrilla forces became known by Americans and South Vietnamese as the Viet Cong.

American military involvement in Vietnam dates from the time those first advisors were sent to help train Diem's forces. By 1960 nearly 700 U.S. military advisers were in place. The insurgency of the Viet Cong increased, and President John F. Kennedy committed another 2,500 troops to Vietnam by the close of 1961. The escalation of American involvement began in earnest when Diem was ousted in a 1963 coup, and the job of stabilizing Saigon and the surrounding areas fell now to more than 16,000 American troops making up the U.S. Military Assistance Command. Lyndon Baines Johnson was entering the White House then, on the heels of President Kennedy's assassination, and the first major battle involving U.S. troops against the Viet Cong and North Vietnamese was about to take place. The fighting would last for more than a decade until the last of the U.S. troops pulled out in 1975. Troop levels under Johnson rose dramatically, with 185,000 American soldiers and sailors in Vietnam by the end of 1965, reaching a peak of 587,000 in 1968. The Vietnam War had essentially become "Americanized" by the Johnson administration following an attack on American barracks at Pleiku in 1965 and a retaliation bombing strike against North Korea following that. That raid became the start of a sustained bombing campaign against the North called Operation Rolling Thunder. Johnson made the decision to expand the ground war, ordering in more troops, and General William Westmoreland was put in charge of the American military operation in Vietnam.

Vietnam was a war like no other the United States had waged, and the role the press played became increasingly important in how the war was conducted, the protest movement in the United States, and eventually the decision to withdraw American troops altogether in 1975. Johnson and his military chiefs found themselves in a dilemma that was seen as a kind of political war trap. Set against the context of the nuclear age, domestic politics in the United States, and the Cold War with Russia, the trap focused on a teetering ally in South Vietnam, whose regime was threatened on all sides. But Johnson worried if South Vietnam fell to the North, then the Communists would have a strong foothold in the Southeast Asian region. That, it was felt, would trigger other Communist takeovers, hence the classic "domino theory" of the U.S. involvement in Vietnam.

To keep the dominos from falling, Johnson felt the only course was increased military action by U.S. troops helping South Vietnam against Communist aggressors. On the other hand, the administration felt they could not use unrestrained military force for fear of involving the United States in a broader superpower confrontation with China or even the Soviet Union. So the decision was made to carry on a kind of ironic grand scale/limited warfare action in Vietnam that would limit itself to conventional military weapons. The goal was to achieve political—as opposed to territorial—objectives. The U.S. government felt it could cause the North Vietnamese enough pain to bring them to the bargaining table in earnest. The Vietnam War (which was officially called a "conflict") became battle after battle of attrition, and it was a matter of who would tire first from all the casualties inflicted. Johnson himself described his position as a middle ground between pulling out and using all-out nuclear warfare to bring North Vietnam to its knees.

Back home, of course, America was being torn apart by protests and ubiquitous demonstrations against the war, its costs, and its aims. The American people gradually began realizing that whatever happened to Vietnam would not be a direct threat to their safety or way of life as Hitler had been in World War II. But the fact that the Selective Service System (the "draft") was in place meant that all young able-bodied men of age 18 and over were directly threatened by the probability that they would end up in Vietnam themselves. The one "out," other than physical disabilities, was staying in school. College students in good standing with their schools could defer their service until after graduation.

The Johnson administration and its generals had to come up with a way of conveying the notion of "progress" in Vietnam to the American people. It was a problem similar to the one President George W. Bush faced in pressing military action against Iraqi insurgents following the takeover of the country in 2004. In Vietnam—as in Iraq—there were few conventional battles and, as mentioned earlier, objectives were not framed in geographical terms such as taking over Hanoi or all ground north of the Seventeenth Parallel. In fact, there were no land objectives involved; only subjective political objectives. So the military decided to develop its own jargon of progress that was put into words like "pacification zones" and "kill ratios." The number of enemy dead was officially always much higher than the number of dead U.S. troops, and that was somehow supposed to be an indicator of progress toward political goals.

As for the press, journalists were allowed to roam where they pleased in Vietnam, and it became the most comprehensively covered war to date. Indeed, it was America's first real "television war." And although there might be a day's delay before footage from the field appeared on American television screens, it was too close to real time for many American television viewers. Watching American soldiers get injured and killed every night as Americans sat down to eat was a shocking experience and brought the raw dimension of war home like never before. The parade of body bags, the sobbing relatives who were interviewed back home, the tapes of American soldiers taken prisoner by the enemy and tortured into making public confessions of American wrongdoing, all of these images fueled the protest in America and put even more pressure on Johnson—and Nixon after him—to bring this war to an end.

It became clear to the Johnson and Nixon administrations that the press was fueling public opinion about the war and that conducting the war under such intense media scrutiny was extremely hard. Again, President Bush discovered the same thing in pressing the Iraqi military action. By November 1967, Johnson's administration began a wide-ranging public relations campaign with the purpose of persuading the press, Congress, and the American public that "progress" did exist in Vietnam and that the war was being "won." The White House media aides began advising LBJ to stress the theme of "light at the end of the tunnel" rather than talking about specific battles, wins, losses, or casualties. As part of this effort to guide the news media into buying into this theme, Johnson brought Westmoreland to Washington, D.C., to address a large gathering of journalists, reporting that America was winning the war and that the end was in sight. This speech was highly publicized, and it seemed for awhile as if much of America was buying the idea, until January 1968 when the North Vietnamese regular army and the Viet Cong launched an all-out offensive (called the "TET" or New Year offensive) against 100 cities in South Vietnam, including Saigon itself. The fury and magnitude of this attack convinced much of America that the war was not being won, and that opinion was even shared by the best-known and most trusted television journalist in America: CBS evening news anchor Walter Cronkite. Upon returning from a fact-finding trip to Vietnam, the venerable Cronkite stepped outside his normal objective role to announce to the nation on his February 27th newscast that ". . .the bloody experience of Vietnam is to end in a stalemate" and that the war was unwinnable. Reports from the White House had President Johnson reacting, "That's it. If I've lost Cronkite, I've lost middle America."

The press coverage itself became more graphic and, once again, the power of visual images shocked the nation as they watched a young Vietnamese girl running naked down a dusty road, screeching as she tried to avoid a napalm attack, and the photo of a Viet cong terrorist captured by South Vietnamese military officials, one of whom put a gun to the man's head and pulled the trigger on camera.

Nevertheless, the war in Vietnam continued for another seven years. Johnson decided not to run for re-election in 1968, and Richard Nixon succeeded him in a landslide vote against Democratic challenger Hubert Humphrey. The Nixon administration continued to press the war in search of "peace with honor," although a gradual troop reduction did take place during Nixon's years, ending with negotiations by Secretary of State Henry Kissinger, which resulted in a total American pullout in 1975. Shortly thereafter, South Vietnam fell to the Communists.

To this date historians still debate whether the American pullout came because of the intense press coverage of the war, and most believe it did. As previous chapters have shown, the press is a big determinant of American public opinion, and this was certainly the case with the Vietnam War. Although the press corps was divided going into the war, with many taking the same orientation they had in World War II of supporting the U.S. cause, a growing number of journalists took a different tack. They became aware that what the government and military were saying, as opposed to what was happening before their eyes in Vietnam, were not one and the same. The so-called "credibility gap" became a favored term to describe the discrepancies, and the daily military briefings in Vietnam became known by the press as "the five o'clock follies." Leading the new breed of journalists in Vietnam were David Halberstam of the New York Times, Neil Sheehan of United Press International, and Malcolm Browne of the Associated Press. Halberstam and Browne shared the Pulitzer Prize for International Reporting in 1964. These and other journalists who reported often on this gap in what the military was saying versus what was really happening were often the target of more traditional journalists in Vietnam. Even *Time* magazine editorially denounced their reporting, saying it undermined the American effort in Vietnam. Later revelations, which surfaced in the so-called "Pentagon Papers" when the *New York Times* published them in 1971, validated most of the coverage by Halberstam, Sheehan, and Browne from 1961–1965. The Pentagon Papers were documents that comprised the contents of a secret analysis done by Pentagon researchers about the reasons for the American involvement in Vietnam and how the war had actually been waged. The Nixon administration feared their publication so much that Attorney General John Mitchell was ordered to file suit against the *New York Times* to suppress publication of the papers. The court denied the motion, however, calling it "prior restraint," which it said was outlawed under the U.S. Constitution.

The lessons that future presidents and military commanders learned from the Vietnam experience helped form the framework of how they would deal with the news media in future U.S. military engagements. Having journalists roam wherever they pleased during combat operations and report whatever they liked have not been seen as helpful in pressing military action since Vietnam. When the United State decided to send troops to Grenada in the Caribbean in 1983 to deal with the threat of a Cuban air base, the press were not allowed to go ashore with the invasion force. Instead, they were kept at bay and were brought ashore after the landing. The same held true for the ensuing skirmishes that took place on the island. Journalists were fed official reports of the "successes" of the military operation which were not supported by future Pentagon post-action reports. The nation's press corps demanded that this censorship arrangement be changed, and the government responded with the "pool" system of allowing groups of certified journalists to go into future battles, usually alongside public affairs officers assigned to each battle unit.

THE FIRST GULF WAR

The first Gulf War, which the Bush administration dubbed Operation Desert Storm, began with the U.S. bombing of Baghdad in January 1991 following months of warnings to Iraq's Saddam Hussein to pull his troops out of Kuwait, the country Iraq invaded on August 2, 1990. Strictly speaking, the first Gulf War was not just a conflict between Iraq and the United States, but between Iraq and a collation force of approximately 20 nations led by the United States under a mandate by the United Nations to liberate Kuwait. American and British correspondents were in Baghdad prior to the January 17, 1991, bombing raid on Baghdad, and most of them tried to get out before the strike began. The only broadcasting crew possessing the means to report live from the scene was the CNN reporting crew led by producer Robert Weiner and correspondents Peter Arnett, John Holliman, and Bernard Shaw. Their transmission means was a small box called a "four wire" that enabled them to broadcast (orally only) live from the scene of the Al Rashid Hotel where the journalists were staying. While other correspondents huddled in the basement of the hotel to avoid the attack, the CNN crew stayed in their upper-floor room, windows open, reporting the bombing raid as it was occurring and hoping the next bomb didn't land on them. For their ingenuity and bravery, the CNN correspondents received numerous accolades from colleagues at ABC, NBC, and CBS, as well as senior U.S. government officials. Even Secretary of Defense Dick Cheney said it was the best American reporting he had witnessed of the operation.

The war was quick and decisive. Preceded by some 1,000 air sorties and using advanced, computer-driven "smart bombs" and cruise missiles, the first goal of the Coalition Force was to destroy the Iraqi air force and anti-aircraft installations. It was followed by the goals of knocking out Iraq's communication infrastructure and then targeting military installations in Iraq and Kuwait. The air campaign was joined in February by a ground campaign, called Operation Desert Sabre, which struck at Iraqi forces in Kuwait. Soon the U.S. VII Corps moved, in full strength, into Iraq itself, and the ground campaign in Iraq was on. Four days later, President Bush announced that Kuwait had been liberated, and a cease-fire was declared. Participating in the brief campaign had been some 550,000 U.S. troops, who were joined by just over 40,000 British troops, about 40,000 Saudi Arabian troops, 35,000 from Egypt, and smaller forces from France, Syria, Kuwait, Canada, and a few other countries.

Press coverage of the first Gulf War was dominated by a pool system put into place by the Pentagon, whereby reporters were credentialed and chosen to accompany certain military units, with public affairs officers assigned to each unit and often present in interviews correspondents did with soldiers. In some cases, journalists broke ranks and chose to go off independently and cover various military actions. Sometimes these reporters were detained by Iraqi forces. One such case was CBS's Bob Simon and his three-member crew, who were taken prisoner for 40 days while reporting outside the system the Pentagon set up. An interesting case was that of Peter Arnett, who chose to stay in Baghdad after all western reporters were ordered out of the country by Iraqi officials. Whether he was actually detained by Iraqis or not was a matter of debate, as were his reports, which CNN chose to carry with the caveat that their degree of objectivity might be suspect since he was reporting under the watchful eye of the Iraqi army. The Bush administration did not receive Arnett's reporting well, since they were hopeful that their rhetoric of "smart bombs" and "surgical precision" would suggest to Americans that this was a low-threat war to Iraqi civilians. Arnett's reports instead showed widespread casualties among Iraq's civilian population. As early as January 25, 1991, the Bush Administration insisted that Arnett was being used as a propaganda tool of the Iraqi army, and some 34 members of Congress contacted CNN executives and accused Arnett of unpatriotic journalism.

One of the unique features of the coverage of the first Gulf War was that this was television's first "real-time" war where, often, live coverage dominated the airwaves, especially on CNN. The hazards of that initially were the unknown element of chemical warfare which Saddam might employ on the battlefield, and the always-worrisome issue of the fog of war as it was being reported live by correspondents. The shrinking amount of time from reporting to broadcasting meant that some rumors paraded themselves as fact and, at times, the reporter on camera just did not know what was going on. To deal with the threat of chemical warfare, much of the early reporting from the Gulf was done by correspondents wearing gas masks on camera.

Because of the short duration of the Gulf War and its quick decisiveness in favor of Coalition forces, protest at home in the United States did not have time to foment to the level of being a factor in how this war was conducted. It was over almost before it began, victory was never in question, American casualties were relatively light, and there was not the nightly parade of body bags that Vietnam had produced month after month, year after year. The question occupying the minds of some in the press by the war's end was whether the war had ended too soon, and whether Coalition forces should have made it their additional objective to remove Saddam Hussein from power. But the Bush administration was adamant that the main goal was to get Iraqi forces out of Kuwait and install a monitoring procedure for weapons of mass destruction that might be developed by Iraq.

THE SECOND GULF WAR

Also known as the Iraq War, this second U.S.-led incursion into Iraq began in March 2003 with another bombing raid against Baghdad and, like the first Gulf War, lasted only about a month. At least, that's how long it took to subdue Iraqi troops and claim Baghdad. The fighting with insurgent groups has lasted years. The impetus of the war lay in the fact that the Iraqi government under

Saddam Hussein failed in its cooperation with teams of United Nations weapons inspectors in the years following the first Gulf War. Also put on the table as a key reason by the George W. Bush administration was intelligence which allegedly "proved" that Saddam had weapons of mass destruction and thus posed a threat to America and the Middle East. Another reason was that Iraq was a state sponsoring terrorism, and the Bush administration claimed there was a link between Iraq and the terrorists who staged the 2001 attack in America known as 9/11. Following those attacks on the World Trade Center and the Pentagon, the U.S. transitioned toward a first-strike doctrine against suspected terrorist and state-supported terrorist sites. U.S.-led forces moved first into Afghanistan after the Taliban forces, then Bush set his sights on Iraq.

This time it was harder for the United States to find significant allies in its military intentions toward Iraq. Strong objections came from France, Russia, and Germany as Bush moved toward war. Turkey refused to let the United States use its territory for a staging area. Bush called upon the U.N. Security Council for specific approval of his military intentions and, although he did not receive it, decided to issue an ultimatum to Saddam Hussein on March 17 to reveal his weapons of mass destruction to inspectors. Two days later the U.S. air strike was launched against Iraq's leadership. The following day the ground campaign, involving significantly fewer troops than the first Gulf War and made up almost entirely of U.S. and British forces, began. The push was towards Baghdad and the southern oil fields and ports, and it was swift. It was joined soon by a northern front as the Coalition forces applied the pliers to squeeze Baghdad into submission. By the middle of April, Saddam's army and his government ceased to exist. On May 1, President Bush declared victory over Iraq in the war. A vexing issue, which became louder as weeks and months wore on, was that no weapons of mass destruction were found by any of the invading U.S. or British troops. Had the Bush administration exaggerated—or even made up—the claims of such weaponry existing? The debate swept America, and slowly President Bush shifted his reasons for going into Iraq, stating that getting rid of Saddam made the world—and especially the Middle East—that much safer. Eventually, Saddam was caught, brought to trial, and executed.

Although the war was swift, the bloody aftermath, wherein more than 2,300 U.S. troops were killed fighting insurgents in Iraq as of 2007. The warning that former Secretary of State Colin Powell issued to President Bush, stating that he would "own" Iraq after the war and he should decide what to do with it, rang true in the months and years to come. Under Secretary of Defense Donald Rumsfeld, the United States continued to establish its presence in Iraq with the avowed aims of training Iraqi security forces to one day take over themselves. A clear goal was to provide security for Iraqi elections and the construction of a constitution. Overall, the stated goal was to bring democracy to Iraq and to give it a chance to take root. The costs, however, continued to mount both in American lives and dollars, and the benefits were seen by many Americans as too dismal. Iraq did not seem to become any safer than before, and the fighting seemed endless as more terrorists and insurgents moved into the country than seemingly existed before the war began. Yes, elections did take place and a constitution was installed. But the country could not be secured in the face of a growing threat of civil war. And, like Vietnam, how long would the American public agree to let its president press a war that was, in large measure, seen as irrelevant to the United States? Probably the one thing that kept the protest from becoming as loud and sustained as Vietnam was the fact that this time it was a volunteer army doing the job; the draft no longer existed, hence the threat of dying in battle was limited to those who chose to enlist. But without a draft, the number of available troops was limited, so soldiers had to be sent back a second and sometimes a third time to the fighting after finishing previous tours of duty.

Despite the administration's best efforts to put a positive face on the war and to ask Americans for patience, the daily media reports focused mostly on the negative aspects of the war: the steady drumbeat of the dead and wounded U.S. troops, the increased fighting in the provinces, the toll on Iraqi civilians, and the questionable results from all of it. Finally, Americans did speak clearly and did so in the midterm elections of 2006, turning control of both the House of Representatives and the Senate to Democrats for the first time in several years. The issue was the Iraq War, and the decision was that the administration was doing a bad job with it. Despite standing solidly behind Rumsfeld as calls for his resignation reached a peak in 2006, the secretary of defense announced his resignation the day after the 2006 midterm elections, which proved disastrous to the Republican administration. Was there to be a new course? Time would tell.

Coverage of the Iraq War featured the same kind of pool system that the military had used in the first Gulf War, although this time selected reporters were "embedded" with fighting troops and had more of a front-line view of combat. This became a controversial situation and was debated by many in the press who worried about the loss of objectivity that embedded reporters might experience. Cut off from their colleagues in the media and put into the middle of an armed fighting unit, could the reporters provide an objective account, or would they become "a part of the team?" Beyond the informal debates, a formal research study was conducted for the BBC by researchers in the School of Journalism, Media and Cultural Studies at Cardiff University in England. The study found that "reporters embedded with military units were generally able to preserve their objectivity, but the practice raised serious causes for concern."[8] The findings were based on interviews with 37 key actors in the broadcast coverage, 27 of whom were reporters, editors, and heads of news departments, and 10 of whom were key personnel with the British Ministry of Defence and the Pentagon. Additionally, a content analysis was performed on the broadcast coverage of the war and, finally, members of the public were questioned in several focus groups about their views on the media coverage of the embedded reporters.

The researchers proclaimed the findings mixed as to reporter objectivity and noted:

> On the one hand, the research found no evidence to support the idea that embeds were necessarily "in bed" with the military or the US/British government in their reporting. While some experienced attempts to censor their reports, the journalists involved made efforts to protect their objectivity, and, on key issues, were demonstrably able to do so. Embedded reports were also often more reliable than reports from official military briefings. The research does, however, raise some serious concerns: Embeds were not able to show the grim side of war, and avoided images they knew would be too graphic or violent for British television. As a result, many viewers felt that the front-line footage provided by embeds was like watching a "war film" rather than capturing the reality of war...Both reporters and viewers strongly support the notion of independent reporting during war, and there are fears amongst journalists that U.S. military strategy will made embedding the only safe option.[9]

Echoing the positive and negative aspects of the "embed" system is Adrian Van Klaveren, head of newsgathering for the BBC, who notes that it makes for compelling television and allows viewers to understand better what is happening on the battlefield.[10] That is different from Gulf War I, where reporters were largely kept at arms length from the fighting and brought in afterwards in pools. "The advantage is that you get to see what's going on at a very localized level. So when we talk about pockets of resistance, viewers can see exactly what we mean," Van Klaveren says.[11] Another advantage is that embedded reporters go into battle under the protection of the armed fighting unit they are assigned to. Several American and British reporters and photojournalists were killed or injured in covering Iraq, and some of them—like ITN's Terry Lloyd, who was killed while pursuing a story on his own—outside the embed system. The downside is, again, the risk to journalistic objectivity. Overall, the relationship between the media and the military is an uneasy one, especially in times of battle. The goals of each institution are different as the military wants to win battles and use the media as helpful propaganda when possible. Journalists, on the other hand, are trying to come up with as honest and candid a view as possible concerning what is actually going on. Sometimes that means knifing through the half-truths that military officials may tell them and deciphering the euphemisms military officials are rattling off. Still, Van Klaveren said there has been no censorship, and reporters have not been required to submit scripts before they aired. A few "golden rules" still exist, however. For example, correspondents are not to divulge details concerning their unit's location in the field, nor outline what their unit plans to do next.[12]

One of the most highly regarded reporters covering the Middle East is CNN's Christiane Amanpour. Interviewed on the 2003 PBS television series, *Reporting America at War*, Ms. Amanpour decried the Pentagon pool system, calling it a kind of "roulette" where reporters were picked by the military for the various pools.[13] In her own case, she was put into a pool on an aircraft carrier in the

Red Sea, far removed from the ground she normally had covered for years. On board the carrier, when the order came for the Navy to strike deep in Iraq in 2003, Amanpour said her adrenaline gave way to the sad reality that she and the other reporters were prevented from asking specific questions of the pilots or other people. Instead, she said, she and the other pool members had to resort to reporting feature stories. And some of those feature stories didn't even pass Naval censors despite the fact they had nothing to do with the actual military operations. Her conclusion about the war coverage was as follows:

> I think the pool system itself was a failure. I think we (correspondents) bear some responsibility for the failure to report the war in full. I think we reported it as accurately as we could have done, but lost a lot of texture. We on the ground pushed very, very hard. Many of my colleagues went around the system, with certain dangerous results (such as Bob Simon's capture)...This had a chilling effect, as you can imagine, on many people. In my view, the restrictions that the military put on us forced some of us to break rules and do things that maybe we wouldn't have done had we had normal access ... I have always got on very well with the commanders, with the soldiers on the ground. There's an element of respect...People get to know which reporters they can trust. When it comes to the public information officers, their brief is from the political side, for the most part. They are concerned 95 percent with image. That's where the balance gets out of whack. That's where we start facing problems as to whether we are being censored and denied access.[14]

One more thing should be noted about the U.S. government's attempt to influence imagery of the Iraq War: the psychological operations unit of the U.S. military was very busy in Iraq. As New York Times reporter Jeff Gerth noted in December 2005:

> The psychological operations unit of the military has 1,200 troops assigned to is operations unit in Fort Brag, NC. The troops turn out what military officers call "truthful messages" in support of America's goals and objectives in Iraq and else-where. But even the military admits the messages are often one-sided and that their American sponsorship remains a hidden fact. "We call our stuff information and the enemy's propaganda," said Col. Jack N. Summer, then the commander of the Fourth Psychological Operations Group, during a tour in June. Even in the Pentagon, "some public affairs professionals see us unfavorably," and inaccurately, he said, as "lying, dirty tricksters." Recently disclosures have surfaced that a Pentagon contractor in Iraq has paid newspapers to run "good news" stories written by American soldiers. Some in Washington say, however, the practice has weakened U.S. credibility. Top military and White House officials have denied knowing about it.[15]

This practice of "planting" good-news stories and of disguising the source of them has caused angst among the journalists reporting the war. Some fear that others in the field might see legitimate journalists as agents of the military rather than independent reporters out for the truth. And the practice has left some Iraqi newspapers and broadcast stations wondering who to believe.

SUMMARY

From first World War to the second Gulf War, the media, the military, and the White House have been involved in a tense and evolving game of chess, each side with its own often-conflicting goals. The question of how to launch and maintain military offensives while under the prying eyes of journalists is one which has always dogged the military and Washington. The reality is that public opinion comes largely from news media depictions of war and the reasons for war. Washington and the military have only so much control over those media stories, and often they find they have no control over them at all. So the war planners have engaged in developing a series of paradigms designed to allow the media to report the wars, but to do it on terms established by the military and Washington. On the media's side, the issue has always been access to the real stories of the war, and that usually means access to the battlefields and the front lines of action. It means being allowed to report in an unfettered fashion, the way they are used to doing other stories as well. History has shown that journalists can be credited with knowing when a story is too revealing and would pose security risks on the battlefield. During World War I and World War II, battlefield reporters often went beyond the censorship guidelines laid down by the military and withheld any information they felt would compromise the Allied cause. That generally unified spirit of patriotism was tested, however, in the jungles of Vietnam when correspondents realized they were either being deceived at times, or at least told only half-truths much of the time. Even with a spirit of independent reporting, however, came the understanding that information can be a powerful and dangerous tool in the hands of the wrong people, so battlefield correspondents often censored their own stories, or embargoed them until a safer time. In Iraq, the practice of keeping reporters at arms length and in pools during the first Gulf War morphed into the "embedded" system of Gulf War II. That practice was both praised and criticized by reporters, but the "embeds" by and large appreciated the access they were given to the battle sites.

Time will tell how Washington and the military incorporate lessons learned from these later wars into the guidelines they set up for future wars. Certainly the real-time coverage that became possible in the first Gulf War is a vexing issue for military planners as they try to walk the line between the issues of military security for their troops and their hoped-for victories, versus providing journalists with access to the action.

CHAPTER 10

The Media as the Fourth Estate

The news media in America occupy a unique position in the dynamics of government and the governed. While not elected by the public, nor appointed and confirmed by the president or Senate, the press in America have—at times—an influence that seems every bit as powerful as the White House, Congress, and Supreme Court. And that influence is protected by the very first amendment to the American Constitution, declaring freedom of the press from prior restraint by the government.

The term "media" itself, coined by the late Marshall McLuhan, hints at some of that uniqueness in that it suggests a go-between, a middleman, possibly a facilitator. The influential part of the media is suggested by historians, philosophers, and even former presidents. It is not that other advanced democracies don't grant their news organizations similar freedoms that the American freedom enjoy, it is just that—partly due to the structure of American government as contrasted with a parliamentary system—America's media are in a unique position to cast the kind of influence that they do.

For example, in a society where both houses of Congress, as well as the chief executive, are popularly elected, and when those elections come with Constitutional regularity every two, four, or six years, the news media pose an agenda for public consideration and action that is not unlike the liturgical calendar of a church. Certain dates signal a change in thinking or action to certain issues and/or behaviors. In political coverage it seems to work like this: The midterm Congressional elections usually signal the popularity of the sitting presidential administration as voters decide whether to give the president more power by voting same-party leaders to the House and Senate, or whether to balance the power of the White House with opposing party leaders. These midterm elections also signal the "official" start of the campaign season for the presidency, then there are two years of political coverage focusing on this horse race to the White House, followed by a "honeymoon" period which sometimes lasts only a couple of months while the new president gets used to his surroundings. This period is followed by predictive stories focusing on how the leadership of the House and Senate might affect the new presidency, followed by a focus on a changing of the guard in the midterm elections, followed by the start of the presidential campaign season again.

GENESIS OF THE TERM

Through it all, the classic role and job of the news media in a democracy is to make sure everyone in Washington plays it straight and governs in the interest of the American people. Hence the "watchdog" philosophy of the news media: the media as the guardians of democracy, defenders of the faith. From the viewpoint of those who see the news media as situated within the model of a pluralist liberal democracy (in a society that allows a social responsibility or libertarian media system), the mass media are often viewed as the *fourth estate* of government. The idea, in America, is that the fourth estate exists separate from the executive, legislative, and judicial estates, and watches over them for the public good and the good of democracy. The term fourth estate is often credited to nineteenth century historian Thomas Carlyle. In Carlyle's thinking, times of chaos demanded heroes who would step in and control the competing forces wreaking havoc in a society. In the view of this historian, only individuals of strength and dynamic character could become the masters of events and serve to direct the spiritual energies of the ideologies they possessed. In a way, he saw the press as one of these heroes. Lecturing in 1840, he noted the importance of writers and seemed to attribute the notion of the fourth estate to eighteenth century statesman and philosopher Edmund Burke when he said:

> Burke said there were Three Estates in Parliament; but, in the Reporters' Gallery yonder, there sat a *Fourth Estate* more important far than they all. It is not a figure of speech, or a witty saying; it is a literal fact,—very momentous to us in these times. Literature is our Parliament too. Printing, which comes necessarily out of Writing, I say often, is equivalent to Democracy: invent Writing, Democracy is inevitable. Writing brings Printing; brings universal everyday extempore Printing, as we see at present. Whoever can speak, speaking now to the whole nation, becomes a power, a branch of government, with inalienable weight in law-making, in all acts of authority. It matters not what rank he has, what revenues or garnitures. the requisite thing is, that he have a tongue which others will listen to; this and nothing more is requisite. The nation is governed by all that has tongue in the nation: Democracy is virtually there.[1]

To Carlyle, the press existed apart from the existing three estates of the aristocracy, House of Commons, and the priesthood. Its job was to explain the workings of these three powerful institutions and, by that public explanation, to involve the citizenry more in the process of government and to let them know what their leaders were doing and how well (or badly) they were doing it. Only by so doing could the people hope to attain their measure of power themselves by retaining the good leaders and ousting the bad.

This theme has been discussed by many other media and government experts down through history. In America, President Thomas Jefferson is often quoted by journalists as a champion of the free press, even though he was often savaged by newspapers during his time in the presidency. Nevertheless, as the following excerpts from his letters show, he saw the press as a vital tool in a democracy and defined it in educational and watchdog frameworks.

Writing to Edward Carrington in 1787, Jefferson said:

> The basis of our governments being the opinion of the people, the very first object should be to keep that right; and were it left to me to decide whether we should have a government without newspapers or newspapers without a government, I should not hesitate a moment to prefer the latter. But I should mean that every man should receive those papers and be capable of reading them.[2]

In a letter to Thomas Cooper in 1802, Jefferson said, "The press [is] the only tocsin of a nation. [When it] is completely silenced...all means of a general effort [are] taken away."[3]

And writing to the French General Lafayette in 1823, Jefferson noted, "The only security of all is in a free press. The force of public opinion cannot be resisted when permitted freely to be expressed. The agitation it produces must be submitted to. It is necessary, to keep the waters pure."[4]

THE THEORY IN ACTION: WATERGATE

The classic case of the Fourth Estate Theory in action occurred, of course, in 1972 when two Washington Post reporters, Bob Woodward and Carl Bernstein, unraveled the cover-up behind the June 17 break-in at the Democratic National Headquarters in the Watergate Hotel and office complex in Washington, D.C. As later evidence showed, the burglars entered the offices to adjust wiretapping equipment they had installed there in a previous break-in the month before. That cover-up conspiracy reached the doors of the Oval Office and resulted in the criminal convictions of forty White House officials and consultants, including two United States attorney generals (Richard Kleindienst, convicted of a misdemeanor, and John Mitchell, convicted of a felony), and the White House chief of staff, Robert Haldeman. Ultimately it brought a Congressional vote to impeach President Richard M. Nixon which led to his resignation the year following his re-election in 1972.

The massive story actually began as a normal burglary arraignment, and might have remained so had it not been for Woodward's keen eye and sense of logic in covering the courthouse proceedings. The young Post reporter who had only recently joined the newspaper noticed some unusual things at that arraignment, among them the following:

- Although the men were charged with burglary, there was no indication anything was actually stolen. Instead, the men were arrested with various telephone bugging devices in their possession.
- The five defendants were all represented by a single attorney, even though none of them had made a phone call following their arrest.
- When each was asked his name and occupation by District Judge John Bohannon, one of them, James McCord, listed his occupation as "security consultant" and said he had worked for the CIA. Another defendant, Bernard Barker, listed his occupation as "anti-communist."

The Post's story the following day reported the facts of the arraignment but stopped short of alleging any connection between the Nixon administration and the break-in. But as Woodward began to investigate further, he noticed curious intersections between McCord and others in the administration like top presidential aide Charles Colson and security consultant Howard Hunt. Joined by fellow reporter Carl Bernstein, the two devoted themselves to probing those intersections, which then led to other connections between the Committee to Re-Elect the President and the burglars. Days turned into weeks, and then months as Woodward and Bernstein reported on their findings. They often seemed to be the only two journalists in the country doing that, while others dismissed the episode as a simple third-rate burglary gone awry by a few extremists. Nevertheless, the two Post reporters, whose stories were closely edited by Managing Editor Ben Bradlee, continued to write front-page stories exposing the connections between the burglary and the Committee to Re-Elect of the President. Finally, on Oct. 10, 1972, they published a story which revealed in detail that the break-in at the Democratic National Headquarters was part of a larger covert campaign to dismantle the president's political opponents, financed by the Committee to Re-Elect and supervised by several of Nixon's closest associates.

Many thought the story would fade and evaporate after Nixon won a landslide re-election in November 1972 over Democratic challenger George McGovern. After all, the conventional wisdom went, why would Nixon have allowed such a break-in and cover-up to take place? The liberal McGovern seemed out of touch with mainstream America and would probably self-destruct no matter what the Republicans did. But Woodward and Bernstein stayed on the story, with the help of Woodward's secret source who he named "Deep Throat," and with the growing interest of other media in Washington, who now realized a story existed that might be closer to the Oval Office than had previously been suspected. Not only were other news media now probing the connections, but a special Senate investigating committee was formed and chaired by Sen. Sam Ervin to look into Nixon's campaign activities. Events reached a crescendo, leading to the April 30, 1973, resignation of Haldeman and Domestic Affairs Advisor John Ehrlichman, and Attorney General Richard Kleindienst for the cascading evidence of their involvement in the cover-up. A few days later, The Washington Post received the Pulitzer Prize for the work of their two intrepid reporters, Woodward and Bernstein. The story ended later that year when Nixon announced his resignation from the presidency, but the story's legacy was imprinted for all time in the annals of watchdog reporting. Woodward's key source, "Deep Throat," would remain anonymous until May 2005, when Mark Felt, the man who ran FBI operations during the Watergate era, identified himself as that source.

THE WATCHDOG MEETS THE BOTTOM LINE

Two decades after President Nixon resigned following the *Washington Post* investigative work, CBS News launched an investigation into another major story: the intentional "spiking" of nicotine in cigarettes by the major tobacco companies to make their products more addictive. Spearheaded by a *60 Minutes* producer, Lowell Bergman, it looked as though this would be another clear-cut case of Fourth Estate Theory in action. What resulted, however, was a case of watchdog reporting encountering the realities of corporate economic theory. Would the watchdog lose its teeth to the bite of corporate economic theory? Had corporate-owned journalism negated the idealism of the Fourth Estate? Here's how this episode in American journalism unfolded, according to a 1999 PBS *Frontline* series entitled, "Smoke in the Eye," which included interviews with the principals in the drama:[5]

In March 1993, Jeffrey Wigand, director of research for Brown & Williamson tobacco company, was fired by the company. He agreed to sign a confidentiality agreement wherein he would not reveal details of the research the tobacco company was involved in. A few months later, Brown & Williamson suspended Wigand's severance pay and health benefits, thinking he had violated terms of that confidentiality agreement. In November, Wigand agreed to sign a tougher severance agreement, and his benefits were reinstated. The tobacco company was unaware, however, he had been subpoenaed to testify before a Justice Department investigation probing Philip Morris Company's "fire-safe" cigarette program. It was this program that caused CBS' *60 Minutes* Producer Lowell Bergman to meet Wigand. Bergman was in receipt of internal Philip Morris documents that needed translating by a tobacco research expert, so he sought out Wigand, who was living in Louisville, Kentucky, in early February 1993. Later that month, ABC's *Day One* newsmagazine produced a story alleging that Philip Morris spiked the nicotine in its cigarettes. It was a story they would later issue an apology for during a break on its highest-profile program, *Monday Night Football*, under pressure from the tobacco giant. The next month, 60 *minutes* aired its story on Philip Morris's "fire safe" cigarette program—research, the story contended, which was killed by Philip Morris for fear of damaging law suits. CBS reportedly paid Wigand an estimated $12,000 for his services as a consultant.

During the next few months, Stanton Glantz, a professor of medicine at the University of California in San Francisco, was sent some 4,000 pages of internal Brown & Williamson documents by an anonymous donor. Shortly afterwards, the Justice Department launched an investigation into the possible perjury by the chief executives of the seven largest tobacco companies who had previously testified in congressional hearings that "nicotine is not addictive," and that they knew of no practices in their companies to spike their cigarettes. Bergman then proposed investigating a story on Brown & Williamson, 60 *Minutes* executives approved it, and Bergman began working on it with Wigand, with CBS and the source working out an indemnification arrangement should Wigand be sued by the tobacco company. Although Wigand agreed to an interview taping with Mike Wallace, another development at CBS threatened to block the whole story: CBS announced that Westinghouse Electric Corp., a company wishing to buy the network, would pay $5.4 billion to do just that. A couple weeks later, ABC issued its on-air apology to Philip Morris. CBS executives worried that running the revealing interview by Wigand, a man whose character was under attack by Brown & Williamson, might wreck the Westinghouse deal and result in a "tortuous interference" lawsuit by the tobacco company, the judgment of which could be huge. CBS lawyers recommended the interview not air, and CBS executives agreed. Don Hewitt, executive producer of 60 *Minutes*, told the National Press Club:

> We have a story that we think is solid. We don't think anybody could ever sue us for libel. There are some twists and turns, and if you get in front of a jury in some states where the people on that jury are all related to people who work in tobacco companies, look out. That's a $15 billion gun pointed at your head. We may opt to get out of the line of fire. that doesn't make me proud, but it's not my money. I don't have $15 billion. That's Larry Tisch [president of CBS].[6]

The next day, the *Wall Street Journal*, with the help of Wigand, reported on two significant internal reports of Brown & Williamson showing it and other big tobacco companies spike nicotine delivery in their cigarettes by adding ammonia-based compounds. More specifically, the reports said that although the tobacco companies may not have actually hiked the nicotine level itself, they did add chemicals that boosted the potency of the inhaled nicotine. The essence of the story was the same as the 60 *Minutes* shelved interview with Wigand would have revealed. The *Journal* took home a 1996 Pulitzer Prize for its story. As if that weren't enough embarrassment for the venerable journalists at 60 *Minutes*, the *New York Times* published a story on November 9 that 60 Minutes caved in to orders from CBS lawyers and executives to shelve the

Wigand interview. Three days later, *60 Minutes* aired an edited version of the Wigand interview but did not identify Wigand. Correspondent Wallace ended the segment stating:

> We at *60 Minutes*—and that's about 100 of us who turn out this broadcast each week—are proud of working here and at CBS News, and so we were dismayed that the managment at CBS had seen fit to give in to perceived threats of legal action against us by a tobacco industry giant. We've broadcast many such investigative pieces down the years, and we want to be able to continue. We lost out, only to some degree on this one, but we haven't the slightest doubt that we'll be able to continue the *60 Minutes* tradition of reporting such pieces in the future without fear or favor.[7]

Later, in an interview with journalist Charlie Rose, Wallace said he regretted the decision to shelve the Wigand interview and acknowledged that *60 Minutes* had "caved in" to tobacco company pressure. On November 17, Westinghouse concluded its purchase of CBS, and the following February *60 Minutes* aired the entirety of the Wigand interview, taped the previous August. By this time, however, Wigand's stinging revelations had already been published by the *Wall Street Journal* and *New York Times*.

This episode in journalistic history was certainly not the only time that a news organization had felt the "chilling effect" of a potentially huge judgment in a threatened lawsuit. As a matter of fact, the phrase "chilling effect" had been around for years prior to the 1990s. Editors and radio and television producers have long been concerned about the potential legal fallout from their stories. However, as the economic stakes of big media have increased over the decades, and as the ownership of these media has been transferred toward public stock-holders, media executives have become more prone to heeding these legal threats. The CBS/big tobacco controversy was just one of the highest profile of these threats, and it was preceded by ABC's decision to submit to legal pressure with its own exposé of tobacco company practices. Many in the journalistic com-munity believe these legal threats have, in effect, leashed the media watchdog. Coupled with the reality that newspaper readers were avoiding longer stories about complex issues, the economic threats of lawsuits and declining readership have made it harder for the media watchdog to have its day. The situation caused Bill Kovach, former editor of the Atlanta Constitution and curator of Harvard's Nieman Foundation to quip, "Today if you had Watergate, you'd first have to check with the marketing department."[8]

OTHER MEDIA PHILOSOPHIES

The Fourth Estate Theory of the media is one of the most popular philosophies regarding the role of the press in a democratic society, but it is certainly not the only one. As was just discussed, there are definite economic threats operating

to curtail the "defender" theory of the news media. Threats of huge lawsuit judgments and the demands of media stockholders for greater profits have sometimes
squelched expensive efforts at discovering the truth of complex situations.
In fact, economics factor into another philosophy of the media in the United
States. This is the so-called "Critical/Cultural Theory." Under this theory, the
elites of American society use the media to strengthen their positions and their
hold on power and influence. Popularly stated, it is often heard in the quip,
"The power of the press belongs to those who own one." The goal of the elite,
under this philosophy, is to dominate the working classes. The elite influence
the media content, which, in turn, keeps the public in line with ideals of the
influential classes in society. One of the problems with this theory, however, is
what to do with historical examples like the media's uncovering of Watergate,
which led to the resignation of the most influential man in America at the time:
the president of the United States. Still, this philosophy has found a home
among many American intellectuals and was one favored by former MIT linguist
and societal critic Noam Chomsky. One of the ideas of this political/economic
theory is that the very nature of capitalism fuels the political, economic, and
media systems toward injustice. Proponents of this philosophy emphasize
marketplace controls, including the control of labor and on profits as the only
goal. Under this theory, it is vital to centralize power in the hands of the rich
and to control information going to the workers. If this sounds like Marxist
thought, it is. The bases of Marxist thought and critical/cultural media theory
are one and the same: control of the masses by the wealthy, using the media as
one of the means.

Even those not buying into critical/cultural theory understand the role of
the marketplace for the news media and individual reporters and editors. For a
long time, editors and producers have known they need to take the readers and
viewers into account when developing story ideas and publishing or airing those
stories. News executives have found themselves walking a tightrope between
cozying up too much to their readers and viewers, pandering to desires for entertainment and escapism, and staying too detached from those readers and viewers,
emitting a sense of arrogance to the people being asked to buy the newspapers
or watch the newscasts. For most products and services in the marketplace,
manufacturers must take the customers into consideration. In fact, product
development usually begins with the needs and desires of the customer. Why,
then, should things be different for the news media? If you consider their stories
and reports as products and services meant for consumption by the media's
customers, why shouldn't editors and producers supply stories those customers
want to read and hear? And, like other products and services, won't the quality
of news stories improve because of customer demand? These are controversial
thoughts, however, among journalists who believe that the nature of the
news "product" is vastly different from any other product imaginable. After
all, journalists say, the media deal in important information and ideas, the
stories conveying this information must be truthful, and editors must have

the freedom and independence to tell these stories apart from any reader or viewer influence.

In an article entitled, "Serving the Public and Serving the Market: A Conflict of Interest?" researcher John McManus uses market theory to test the assertion that serving the market helps insure that newspapers serve the public as well. McManus concludes:

> The analysis concludes that news is a peculiar commodity—what economists call a "credence" good—that may invite fraud because consumers cannot readily determine its quality, even after consuming it. News, by definition, is what we don't yet know Advertisers seek public attention for their products rather than public education about current events. Thus, advertiser-supported news media, following market logic, compete not in a news market but in a larger market for public attention. This attention market may value entertainment more than information, leading to a conflict with journalism's norms of public service.[9]

McManus feels that market theory, or microeconomics, predicts that for most commodoties, market forces push quality up and prices down. That creates wealth for both buyers and sellers.[10] But he notes a major flaw in the reasoning of those who assert that news media that do a good job of serving the market also best serve the public: the assumption that news media serve a news market at all. As his above conclusion states, the media serve more as a market for public attention than for news. A viewer who watches the evening newscast for entertainment, weather, or sports counts just as much on the Nielsen People Meter as a viewer who watches to be educated or informed. The same holds true for a newspaper subscriber who buys the newspaper only to read the ads, or the comics, or to do the crossword puzzle, who counts as much as the subscriber who buys it to read the news.

SUMMARY

The classic liberal democratic ideal of the media as the "fourth estate" views the media as defenders of the democracy, a task they undertake when they assume the role of a society's watchdog. Numerous examples in American history, including the Watergate series of stories which resulted in the resignation of President Richard M. Nixon, point to the existence of this role and to its significance in American society. However, as popular as the "Fourth Estate Theory" is in democratic societies, it is not the only way in which the news media are viewed. Some critics see the media more as lapdogs than watchdogs, institutions who serve the rich and powerful in a capitalistic, market-driven society. The role of these media, contrary to the belief of "Fourth Estate" theorists, is to control society and bring it in line with the thinking and ideals of the wealthy and influential: society's elite. The reality of daily news media production is that the institution of journalism does not exist in a setting of absolute freedom. Controls arise at times such as the chilling effect of a lawsuit and the economic realities of serving the marketplace that can put a leash on the watch-dog, inhibiting its movement in the arena of investigative reporting. Finally, market theory research indicates that market forces do not necessarily result in a better media product, as those forces might with other types of products and services.

Notes

CHAPTER 1

1. Dana Priest and Anne Hull, "Soldiers Face Neglect, Frustration at Army's Top Medical Facility," *Washington Post*, February 18, 2007, A1.

2. David S. Cloud, "General is Fired over Conditions at Walter Reed, *The New York Times*, March 2, 2007, 1A.

3. Wilson P. Dizard, *Digital Diplomacy: U.S. Foreign Policy in the Information Age* (Westport: Praeger, 2001), 10.

4. Rush Limbaugh, "Bush and New Media Win Huge Victory: Historical Shift Has Taken Place," http://www.rushlimbaugh.com, November 3, 2004.

5. "News Anchors on Right Wing Pressure," Al Franken Show Blog, August 9, 2004, http://www.airamerica.com.

6. Ibid.

7. Lance Morrow, http://www.airamerica.com

8. Ellen Hume, "The Media Circus Begins," July 26, 2004, www.medianation.umb.edu.

9. James Boylan, "The CNN Effect: The Myth of News, Foreign Policy and Intervention," *Columbia Journalism Review*, March/April 2003.

10. David D. Perlmutter, *Photojournalism and Foreign Policy: Icons of Outrage in International Crises* (Westport: Praeger, 1998), 4.

11. Perlmutter, 1.

12. Perlmutter, 11–18.

13. Patrick O'Hefferman, *Mass Media and American Foreign Policy* (Westport: Ablex, 1991), 2–3.

14. Ibid.

15. Dizard, 11.

CHAPTER 2

1. All American Talent and Celebrity Network, http://www.allamericanspeakers.com/newspeakerbio/3333.

2. Pew Research Center for the People and the Press, *Public's news habits little changed since September 11*, retrieved from http://people-press.org/reports.

3. Pew Research Center for the People and the Press, *Cable and Internet loom large in fragmented politically news universe*, retrieved from http://people-press.org/reports.

4. Dr. Geoffrey Baym, "Political news for the Hip-Hop Generation: MTV and the 2004 Presidential Election," 3–4, presented to the NCA Central States Regional Convention in April 2006, Indianapolis, Indiana.

5. Ibid., 10.

6. Ibid., 17.

7. Ibid, 20.

8. *Montgomery Advertiser*, Nov. 20, 2005.

9. Sheila Kaplan, "Covering 9/11," *Columbia Journalism Review*, September 1, 1998 , 37.

10. Drew Wilton, "Political Advertising," *Mother Jones online*May 2000, http://www.motherjones.com.

11. *Brill's Content*, September 1, 1998.

12. Project for Excellence in Journalism, http://www.journalism.org.

13. Bill Carter and Jacques Steinberg, "Anchor-Advocate on Immigration Wins Viewers," *New York Times*, March 29, 2006.

14. Larry King Live, CNN, June 06, 2006.

15. Howard Kurtz. *Spin Cycle: Inside the Clinton Propaganda Machine* (New York: Free Press, 1998), 121–122.

16. Humphrey Taylor, Harris Poll No. 14: "PAC Money, Big Companies, News Media, Political Lobbyists All Seen By Large Majorities as Having Too Much Power and Influence in Washington, D.C.," February 24, 1999, as accessed on http://www.harrisinteractive.com.

CHAPTER 3

1. John C. Merrill, *Global Journalism: Survey of International Communication*, (White Plains: Longman, 1995), xvi.

2. Ibid., xv.

3. Ibid., xvii.

4. John Milton, *Areopagitica*, George Sabine, ed. (new York: Appleton, 1951), 50.

5. Ibid., 6.

6. Michael Emery, Edwin Emery, and Nancy L. Roberts, *The Press and America: An Interpretive History of the Mass Media* (Boston: Allyn and Bacon, 2000), 12.

7. Ibid.

8. Ibid., 14–15.

9. Samuel Adams, *The Boston Gazette*, August 19, 1771, as quoted in "Legacy of Sam Adams," by William James Willis, Nieman Reports, summer 1984, 24.

10. Emery, et al, 49–50.

11. Ibid.

12. Thomas Paine, *Crisis*, as quoted in *The Press and America: An Interpretive History of the Mass Media* (Boston: Allyn & Bacon, 2000), 56.

13. Fred Siebert, Theodore Peterson, and Wilbur Schramm, *The Four Theories of the Press* (Urbana: Illini Books, 1963).

14. *Commission on Freedom of the Press, as found in the Ruth A. Inglis Papers on the Commission on Freedom of the Press, 1944-48*, Manuscript Collection 0078, George Washington University Library, Washington, D.C.

15. Reporters Without Borders', *Annual World Press Freedom Index of 2005*.

16. Ibid.

17. International Commission for the Study of Communication Problems, UNESCO, *Many Voices, One World* (Paris: UNESCO, 1980), 253–75.

18. Letter from George P. Schultz, Secretary of State, United States of America, Washington, D.C., to the Honorable Amadou-mahtar M'Bow, Director General, United Nations Educational, Scientific and Cultural Organization, Paris, December 28, 1983; letter reprinted in the *Journal of Communication* 34 (Autumn 1984), 82.

19. Memorandum from William G. Harley, communications consultant, United States State Department, Washington, D.C., February, 9, 1984, revised April 1984; reprinted in the *Journal of Communication* 34 (Autumn 1984), 89.

20. Johan Galtung and Richard C. Vincent, *Global Glasnost: Toward a New World Information and Communication Order?* (Cresskill: Hampton Press, 1982), 94. In part this passage quotes Leonard R. Sussman, "World Forum: The U.S. Decision to Withdraw from UNESCO," *Journal of Communication* 34 (Autumn 1984), 159.

21. "Old World Information Order," *The Nation*, July 7–14, 1984, 6–7.

22. Galtung and Vincent, 104.

CHAPTER 4

1. Herbert J. Gans, *Deciding What's News* (New York: Vintage Books, 1978).

2. Simon Cottle, ed., *News, Public Relations, and Power*, (Thousand Oaks: Sage, 2003).

CHAPTER 5

1. "Columbine families sue computer game makers," http://News.BBC.co.uk.

2. "Violence Assessment Monitoring Project (1995-1998)," UCLA Center for Communication Policy in the School of Public Policy and Social Research, Los Angeles, California.

3. Glen Sparks, *Media Effects Research: A Basic Overview (2nd ed.)* (Belmont, MA: Thomson/Wadsworth, 2006), 176.

4. Spiro Kiousis, Ph.D., "Agenda-Setting and Voter Turnout among Youth: Implications for Political Socialization," University of Florida, in a paper presented to the Association for Education in Journalism and Mass Communication annual convention, San Francisco, California, August 2006, 1.

5. Ibid.

6. Margaret Gerteis, "Violence, Public health, and the Media," based on the conference "Mass Communication and Social Agenda-Setting" convened by the Annenberg Washington Program and the Center for Health Communication of the Harvard School of Public Health, Oct. 20–21, 1993.

7. Ibid.

8. Ibid.

9. Ibid.

10. Ibid.

11. Ibid.

12. Ibid.

13. *Construction of Saudi Arabia's Social Reality Before and After September 11, 2001 by U.S. Mainstream Television News Oraganizations in Relation to U.S. Government Officials'*

News Framing. A dissertation by Abulrahman Abdullah Al-Zuhayyan, University of Memphis, Memphis, Tennessee, May 2006, iv.

14. Ibid.

15. Al-Zuhayyan, 2–3.

16. Al-Zuhayyan, 4.

17. 17. Ibid.

18. Fred Vultee, "Agenda for trouble: News frames of mitigation and responsibility after Hurricane Katrina," University of Missouri, a paper presented to the Association for Education in Journalism and Mass Communication annual convention, San Francisco, California, August 2006.

19. Vultee, 2–3.

20. Vultee. 14.

21. Ibid.

22. John Ryan and William M. Wentworth, *Media and Society: The Production of Culture in the Mass Media,* (Boston: Allyn & Bacon, 1999), 67–68.

23. William P. Eveland, Jr., "The Benchwarmers Hit a Home Run: Non-Traditional Political Communication Effects in 2004," Ohio State University, in a paper presented to the Association for Education in Journalism and Mass Communication annual convention, San Francisco, California, August 2006, 2.

24. Eveland, 3.

25. Eveland, 10.

26. Jim Willis, *The Shadow World: Life Between the News Media and Reality,* (Westport, CT: Praeger, 1991), 226.

CHAPTER 6

1. David Weaver, Randal Beam, Bonnie Brownlee, Paul S. Voakes, and G. Cleveland Wilhoit, "Indiana University School of Journalism American Journalist Survey: The Face and Mind of the American Journalist," http://www.poynter.org, April 10, 2003.

2. Herbert J. Gans, *Deciding What's News* (New York: Vintage Books, 1978).

3. Jim Willis, *The Editor as a People Manager,* unpublished doctoral dissertation at the University of Missouri, Columbia, Missouri, 1982.

4. Sebastian Junger, *The Perfect Storm.*(New York: HaperCollins, 1997), IX and X.

5. Tim Jones, "The Day of the Analysts: Wall Street and the Future of Newspapers," *Columbia Journalism Review*, November/December 1996, 42.

6. Daniel Boorstin, *The Image: A Guide to Pseudo-Events in America,* (New York: Vintage, 1992), 9–12.

7. Richard Critchfield, "The Village Voice of Richard Critchfield," *Washington Journalism Review*, October 1985, 28.

8. John Leo, "Spicing up the (ho-hum) truth," *US News and World Report*, March 8, 1993, 24.

9. Rachel L. Swarns, "Dobbs's Outspokenness Draws Fans and Fire," *New York Times*, Feb. 15, 2006, B1 and B4.

10. Larry King Live, interview with Anderson Cooper, June 6, 2006, CNN.

11. Jaap van Ginneken, *Understanding Global News: A Critical Introduction* (Thousand Oaks, CA: Sage, 1998), 144.

12. vanGinneken, 159.

13. vanGinneken, 161.

CHAPTER 7

1. Barack Obama, keynote address of the Democratic National Convention, July 27, 2004.

2. Bob Schieffer, *This Just In: What I couldn't Tell you on TV* (New York: G.P. Putnam, 2003), 227.

3. Mike Boettcher, in comments to a seminar on "Terrorists and the Media," November 3, 2001, University of Memphis, Memphis, TN.

4. *The Press and America: An Interpretive History of the Mass Media*, 9th ed. (Boston: Allyn & Bacon, 2000), 67.

5. "Illusions of News," a segment of the series, *The Public Mind*, airing on PBS and produced by WGBH, Boston, November 1989.

6. Howard Kurtz, *Spin Cycle: Inside the Clinton Propaganda Machine* (New York, Free Press, 1998), 15.

7. *Spin Cycle*, 106.

8. *Spin Cycle*, 108.

9. *Spin Cycle*, 110.

CHAPTER 8

1. *The Harper Book of Quotations*, 3rd ed., Robert I. Fitzhenry, ed. (New Yotk: HarperCollins, 1993), 319.

2. Dan Rather with Mickey Herskowitz, *The Camera Never Blinks* (New York: Ballantine, 1978), 162–164.

3. James Pollard, *Presidents and the Press* (Washington D.C.: Public Affairs Press, 1964), 383–384.

4. William C. Spragens, *From Spokesman to Press Secretary* (Lanham, MD: University Press of America, 1980), 84.

5. Helen Thomas, *Dateline: White House* (New York: Macmillan, 1975), 281.

6. Joseph C. Spear, *Presidents and the Press* (Cambridge: MIT Press, 1984), 200–201.

7. Pollard, 24.

8. Pollard, 7.

9. Pollard, 12.

10. Richard Nixon, *RN* (New York: Grosset & Dunlap, 1978), 245.

11. Bob Schieffer, *This Just In: What I Couldn't Tell you on TV* (New York: G.P. Putnam, 2003), 216.

12. Schieffer, 246.

13. Schieffer, 247.

14. Schieffer, 249.

15. CBS Transcript of January 25, 1988, interview by Dan Rather of Vice President George H.W. Bush, as contained inDavid Corn, "When Dan Rather Tried to Hold a Bush Accountable," published on March 11, 2005, on http://www.commondreams.org and accessed through that web site. Also available at http://www.ratherbiased.com/transcript.htm.

16. "Illusions of News," a segment of the PBS series, *The Public Mind*, produced by WGBH and aired in November 1989.

17. W. Dale Nelson, *Who Speaks for the President?* (Syracuse: Syracuse University Press, 1998), 248.

18. Nelson, 250.

19. Ibid.

CHAPTER 9

1. A *Treasury of Great Reporting*, Louis L. Snyder and Richard B. Morris, eds. (New York: Simon and Schuster, 1962), 275.

2. Michael Emery, Edwin Emery, and Nancy L. Roberts, *The Press and America: An Interpretive History of the Mass Media*, 9th ed. (Boston: Allyn and Bacon, 2000), 254.

3. Walter Lippmann, *Public Opinion*. (New York: Macmillan, 1922), 13.

4. Walton E. Bean. "The Accuracy of Creel Committee News, 1917-1919: An Examination of Cases," *Journalism Quarterly*, XVIII (September 1941), 272.

5. Emery, et al, 256.

6. William L. Shirer, as quoted in Jim Willis, *The Shadow World: Life Between the News Media and Reality*, (Westport, CT: Praeger, 1991), 47.

7. Emery, et al., 410.

8. Justin Lewis, Terry Threadgold, Rod Brookes, Nick Mosdell, Kirsten Brander, Sadie Clifford, Ehab Bessaiso and Zahera Harb, "Mixed verdict on Iraq 'embedded' reporters." Cardiff University Public Relations Office, November 6, 2003.

9. Ibid.

10. "How 'embedded' reporters are handling the war," http://News.BBC.co.uk, March 25, 2003.

11. Ibid.

12. Ibid.

13. *Reporting America at War: An Oral History*, compiled by Michelle Ferrari, with commentary by James Tobin, Goodhue Pictures, 2003.

14. Ibid.

15. Ibid.

CHAPTER 10

1. Quoted from Thomas Carlyle, "The Hero as Man of Letters: Johnson, Rousseau, Burns," Lecture V, May 19, 1840, Edinburgh, Scotland.

2. *The Writings of Thomas Jefferson*, Memorial Edition edited by Lipscomb and Bergh, Vol. 6:57, New York, 1892–99.

3. Lipscomb and Bergh, Vol. 10:341.

4. Lipscomb and Bergh, Vol. 15:491.

5. "Smoke in the Eye: Why Did CBS and ABC back off from expose's on the tobacco industry?" Public Broadcasting System *Frontline* series airing in 1999. Accessed on www.pbs.org/wgbh, November 23, 2006.

6. Ibid.

7. Ibid.

8. Jim Willis, "The Tyranny of the Apathetic," Nieman Reports, Winter, 1991, 12.

9. John McManus, "Serving the Public and Serving the Market: A Conflict of Interest?" Journal of Mass Media Ethics, 7, no. 4 (1992); 198–99.

10. Ibid.

Selected Bibliography

Baum, Matthew A. *Soft News Goes to War: Public Opinion and American Foreign Policy in the New Media Age*. Princeton, NJ: Princeton University, 2003.

Bennett, W. Lance. *Taken by Storm: The Media, Public Opinion, and U.S. Foreign Policy in the Gulf War*. Chicago: University of Chicago, 1994.

Bly, Theresa. *Impact of Public Perception on US National Policy: A Study of Media Influence in Military and Government Decision Making*. Washington D.C.: Storming Media, 2002.

Boorstin, Daniel J. *The Image: A Guide to Pseudo-Events in America*. New York: Atheneum, 1985.

Cottle, Simon. *News, Public Relations, and Power*. Thousand Oaks: Sage, 2003.

Emery, Michael, Edwin Emery, and Nancy L. Roberts. *The Press and America: An Interpretive History of the Mass Media*. 9th ed. Boston: Allyn & Bacon, 2000.

Entman, Robert M. *Projections of Power: Framing News, Public Opinion, and U.S. Foreign Policy*. Chicago: University of Chicago, 2003.

Franklin, Bob, ed. *Social Policy, the Media and Misrepresentation*. London: Routledge, 1999.

Gans, Herbert J. *Deciding What's News*. New York: Vantage, 1980.

Gilens, Martin. *Why Americans Hate Welfare: Race, Media, and the Politics Of Antipoverty Policy*. Chicago: University of Chicago, 2000.

Hausman, Carl. *The Decision Making Process in Journalism*. Chicago: Nelson-Hall, 1987.

Jamieson, Kathleen Hall, and Paul Waldman. *The Press Effect: Politicians, Journalists, and the Stories That Shape the Political World*. Oxford University Press, 2003.

Lippmann, Walter. *Public Opinion*. New York: Macmillan, 1922.

Newman, Jay. *The Journalist in Plato's Cave*. Rutherford, NJ: Fairleigh Dickinson, 1989.

O'Heffernan, Patrick. *Mass Media and American Foreign Policy*. Westport, CT: Ablex, 1991.

Perlmutter, David. *Photojournalism and Foreign Policy*. Westport, CT: Praeger, 2001.

Robinson, Piers. *The CNN Effect: The Myth of News Media, Foreign Policy And Intervention*. London: Routledge, 2002.

Ryan, John, and William M. Wentworth. *Media and Society: The Production of Culture In The Mass Media*. Boston: Allyn & Bacon, 1999.

Sabatier, Paul A., ed. *Theories of the Policy Process*. Boulder, CO: Westview, 1999.

Sparks, Glenn G. *Media Effects Research: A Basic Overview*. 2nd ed. Belmont, MA: Thomson, 2006.

Willis, Jim. *The Human Journalist: Reporters, Perspectives, and Emotions*. Westport, CT: Praeger, 2003.

Willis, Jim. *Reporting on Risks: The Practice and Ethics of Health and Safety Communication*. Westport, CT: Praeger, 1997.

Willis, Jim. *The Shadow World: Life Between the News Media and Reality*. Westport, CT: Praeger, 1990.

Index

2000 presidential election, 116
24-hour news networks, 25
60 Minutes, 47
9/11, 9, 57, 64, 65, 131
access to the president, 106
Adams, Samuel, 6, 30, 32–33
Addison, Joseph, 30–31
advertising in politics, 24
agenda-setting, 51–53, 58–62, 65–67
agitator role of media, 29
Agnew, Spiro T., 5
Aguillera, Christina, 20
AIDS story, 61–62
Al Jazeera, 12, 30, 42, 41
Al Rashid Hotel, 129
Alabama Improper, 23
al-Adon Hospital, 2
All the President's Men, 78
Alliance for Better Campaigns, 24
alternative weeklies, 99
Al-Zuhayyan, Abdulrahman, 64
Amanpour, Christiane, 133–134
America First Committee, 121
American Press Institute, 49
American Society of Newspaper Editors, 25
anecdotal lead, 90
Areopagitica, 31, 33
Arnett, Peter, 7, 129–130
Arsenio Hall Show, 69
ASNE Canons of Journalism, 36
Associated Press, 50–51
attribution frame, 66
Audience Research and Development, 50
authoritarian system of media, 34–35

Baghdad bombing, 56
Balkan incident, 118
Balkans Crisis, 7
Bao Dai, 124–125
Barrymore, Drew, 20
Basketball Diaries, 57
Baym, Geoffrey, 19
BBC Study of embedded journalists, 132–133
Bergman, Lowell, 141
Bernstein, Carl, 5, 78, 139–141
Blair, Jayson, 77
bloggers, 22–23
Boettcher, Mike, 97
Boston Phoenix, 99
bottom-line journalism, 80–81
Bowling for Columbine, 15
Bradlee, Ben, 78, 140
Brokaw, Tom, 19
Brown and Williamson Tobacco, 47–48, 141, 142
Browne, Malcolm, 128
Bush, George H.W., 112–115
Bush, George W., 2, 116, 131–132
Bush-Rather interview, 112–115

Campaign to Ban Land Mines, 2
Capote, Truman, 80
Carlyle, Thomas, 138
Carnegie Endowment for International Peace, 118
Carter, Jimmy, 110–111
Cato's Letters, 32
Chappaquiddick River, 3
Chernobyl, 11

chilling effect of litigation, 47
China and the media, 36–39
Chomsky, Noam, 6, 144
Choose or Lose, 19
Church Peace Union, 118
Citizens for a Free Kuwait, 3
Clinton, Bill, 3, 17, 69, 100–102, 115, 116
Clinton, Hillary, 17, 21, 94
CNN Effect, 7
CNN, 7, 25, 129–130
Code of Wartime Practices, 122
cognitive learning theory, 6
Columbine shooting, 57
commentator popularity, 25–26
Commission on Freedom of the Press, 34–35
Committee on Public Information, 7, 119–120, 122
Committees of Correspondence, 6, 32
Communist Party of China, 37–38
community journalism standards, 85–87
compression effect, 91
conflict in stories, 69
conflictive social reality, 64
contextual accuracy, 87–88
Cooke, Janet, 77
Cooper, Anderson, 25–26, 84–85
credibility gap, 128
Creel, George, 119–120
Critchfield, Richard, 82
criteria of news value, 44–47
critical cultural theory, 6, 144
Cronkite, Walter, 83, 127
C-SPAN, 25
cushion of time, 8, 12

Daily Kos, 22
Davis, Gray, 69
Davis, Richard Harding, 118
Davis, Elmer, 122
Day, Benjamin, 99
deadline pressure, 8
Dean, Howard, 21
Deaver, Michael, 97, 100
Deciding What's News, 75
Deep Throat, 140–141

DeFoe, Daniel, 31
Diena, 39
diplomatic "channel," 7
Dizard, Wilson, 12
Dobbs, Lou, 25–26, 83
domino theory of Vietnam, 125
Donaldson, Sam, 110–111

eastern liberal media establishment, 5
Edes, Benjamin, 33
editorializing in stories, 91–92
Ehrlichman, John, 141
Eisenhower, Dwight D., 108–109, 122
Emanuel, Rahm, 102
embedded journalists 132, 133, 135
emotional journalism, 84–85
enduring values, 75
Espionage Act, 120
Eurosat, 12
Eveland, William P., 68

Face the Nation, 97
Facebook, 21
Family and Medical Leave Act, 102
Fahrenheit 9/11, 15
feasibility of news coverage, 47–48
feed the beast, xii
Fenno, John, 98
films about politics and media, 15–17
fire-safe cigarette, 141
Fitzgerald, Peter, 95
five o'clock follies, 128
Flags of our Fathers, 123
Food Lion story by ABC, 48
Ford, Gerald, 110
fourth estate defined, 138–139
four-wire, 129
Fox News Channel, 25
frame of subjects, 11
Frank Magid and Associates, 50
Franken, Al, 17
Franklin, Benjamin, 30–31
Freneau, Philip, 98

gatekeepers, 43, 74
Gazette of the United States, 98
Gerteis, Margaret, 61

gift-wrapped stories, 48
Gill, John, 33
Glass, Stephen, 77–78
Goddess of Liberty, 6
Gordon, Thomas, 30, 32
Gore, Al, 24, 94, 116
government leaks, 48–49
Grace, Nancy, 94
graphic coverage of Vietnam, 127
Guiliani, Rudolph, 27

Halberstam, David, 128
Haldeman, Robert, 139
Hansen, Jon, 94
Harding, Warren G., 108
Harris, Eric, 56
Hayakawa, S.I., 33, 91
Hearst, William Randolph, 120
Herbert J. Gans, 75
Hewitt, Don, 142
Hill & Knowlton, 3
Hip Hop Politics, 20
Hitler, Adolph, 120–121
Ho Chi Minh, 124
Holliman, John, 129
Hoover, Herbert, 106
horse-race coverage, 97
hot news topics, 50
Hull, Anne, 1
Humphrey, Hubert H., 127
Hundt, Reed, 24
Hurricane Katrina, 57, 65–67
Hussein, Saddam, 129, 130–131
Hutchins, Robert Maynard, 35–36

icons of outrage, 10
images in media, 6
importance of events, 11
imposed trauma, 55
inferences, 91
InstaPundit, 22
Intelsat, 12
internet censorship in China, 38
interpretation, 88
interpretive reporting, 35
inverted pyramid, 9, 69, 89
investigative journalism, 79

Iran hostage crisis, 111
Iran-Contra, 112–115
Iraq War coverage, 130–134
Iwo Jima, 123

Jefferson, Thomas, xii, 35, 105, 139
Jennings, Peter, 5
Johnson, Lyndon Baines, 105–106, 125–126
journalists as citizens, 76–77
journalists of color, 75
judgment language, 91
Junger, Sebastian, 80

Kennedy, John F., 109, 125
Kennedy, Ted, 3
Kerry, John, 21
Keyes, Alan, 95
Kiousis, Spiro, 59–60
Kissinger, Henry, 127
Klebold, Dylan, 57
Kleindeist, Richard, 139–141
Kopechne, Mary Jo, 4
Korean Conflict, 124
Kuwait invasion, 2, 129

Larry King Live, 27, 68
Latvian media, 38–39
League of Nations, 120
Leno, Jay, 28, 68
Letterman, David, 28, 56, 68
Levin, Blair, 24
liberal media critiques, 4
libertarian system of media, 34–35
Life magazine, 123
Limbaugh, Rush, 5, 68
Lindbergh, Charles A., 121
Lippmann, Walter, xi, 119
literary journalism, 79–80
Living History, 17
Look Magazine, 123
LTV, 39
Lusitania, 118
lying among journalists, 77

MacArthur, Douglas, 122
Maher, Bill, 28

market theory of the news, 145
Massachusetts Spy, 33
McBride Commission, 40–41
McCain, John, 27, 94
McClure, S.S., 61
McCord, James, 140
McCurry, Mike, 7, 100–101, 116
McGovern, George, 140
McLuhan, Marshall, 8
McManus, John, 145
media agenda, 65
media congruency construction frame, 64
media consultants, 50
mediated reality, 70–71
medical malpractice series, 47
medical treatment of soldiers, 1
medium is the message, 8
Meet the Press, 94, 97
Memphis Flyer, 99
Merrill, John C., 29
metonymy, 11
Mexican immigration, 4
Middle-East Watch, 3
military censorship, 122–123
Milton, John, 30, 31, 33
Mist's Journal, 31
Mitchell, John, 128, 139
mitigation frame, 66
Moonves, Leslie, 24
Moore, Michael, 15
motivations for journalists, 76–77
Mount Suribachi flag raising, 124
Moyers, Bill, 19
MSNBC, 25
MTV political coverage, 18–20
Murrah Federal Building bombing, 94
Murrow, Edward R., 84
My Life, 17
Myers, Dee Dee, 115
MySpace, 21

name recognition, 93
narrative style, 69, 90
National Association of Broadcasters, 28
National Gazette, 98
National Liberation Front, 125
Nayirah, 2

network news ratings, 25
New Republic, 17, 77
New York Sun, 99
News Corp, 12
news framing, 69–70
news hole, 53
Nixon, Richard M., 5, 106, 109–110,
    127–128, 139, 145
non-traditional media effects, 68–69
NWICO, 35, 41–42

O'Reilly, Bill, 17, 25, 83
Obama, Barack, 94–96
Office of Censorship, 122
Office of War Information, 122
Official Secrets Act, 52
Oklahoma City bombing, 57
Operation Desert Storm coverage, 129–
    130
opinion journalism, 83–84
Oprah Winfrey, 28, 56, 94
Osama Bin Laden, 51

P Diddy, 19–20
Paine, Thomas, 30, 33
Paper Lion, 79
partisan press era, 97–99
party affiliation of journalists, 74
PDA's, 12
peace with honor, 127
Pearl Harbor attack, 122
Pentagon Papers, 128
People's Political Consultative
    Conference, 37
Perlmutter, David, 10–11
personal frame, 66
perspectives of journalists, 79–85
Pew Center Media Consumption Study
    of 2004, 68–69
Pew Center Study on 2004 Elections, 19
photo-ops of president, 100
planting good news, 134
Plato's Republic, 10
Plimpton, George, 79
plumbers unit, 49
political action committees, 27–28
Politicalmoneyline.com, 28

Pollard, James, 108
pool system of media coverage, 128–129, 132
Powell, Jody, 102, 111
Poynter Institute of Media Studies, 49
press conferences of presidents, 106–107
Price, Byron, 122
Priest, Dana, 1
primordality, 11
profit pressure on news media, 74
Project for Excellence in Journalism, 25
pseudo-news, 81
psychological effect of media, 55–56
psychological operations unit of military, 134
public affairs programs on TV, 18
public interest requirements of FCC, 24
Public Opinion, 119
public opinion, 62–65
puppeteer government, 51–53

Rather, Dan, 5, 19, 105–106
raw opinion to public judgment, 63
Reagan, Ronald, 111–112
report language, 91
Reporters Without Borders 2006 Report, 38
Republika, 39
Richardson, Bill, 21
Riverfront Times, 99
Rivington, James, 33
Roosevelt, Franklin D., 106, 108, 121, 123
Rosenthal, Joe, 123
Rumsfeld, Donald, 131

Sarajevo market massacre, 2
Saudi Arabia and U.S. media, 64–65
scene-setting lead, 90
Schieffer, Bob, 97, 110–111
Schramm, Wilbur, 30
Schwarzenegger, Arnold, 69
seaport security, 2
SEATO, 125
Sedition Act, 120
Selective Service System, 126
sensation of the moment, 66

Shaw, Bernard, 129
Shirer, William L., 121
Simpson, O.J., 26–27
smart bombs, 129
Smoke in the Eye, 141
social responsibility system of media, 34–36
socialization of journalists, 49–50
Society of Professional Journalists, 25
soldier's journalism, 120
Sons of Liberty, 6
Soviet-communistic system of media, 34–36
Space Media Network, 11–12
Spear, Joseph, 107
stand-ups of reporters, 92
Stars and Stripes, 120
Steele, Richard, 30–31
Stephanopoulos, George, 115
Stewart, Jon, 19, 28
stimulating effect of media, 56
striking composition, 11
structure of story, 89–91
summary lead, 9, 90
Surgeon General's Workshop on Violence and Public Health, 57
Sway, 20

Tatler and Spectator Essays, 31
terHorst, Jerald, 110
TET Offensive, 127
Thailand and the media, 39–40
Thailand coup, 39
The American Journalist, 74
The Insider, 47
The Nation, 17
The Perfect Storm, 80
The Rise and Fall of the Third Reich, 121
The Year of Living Dangerously, 52
Third World media, 39–42
Thomas, Isaiah, 6
Tiananmen Square, 6, 10, 37
Time magazine, 128
Trading with the Enemy Act, 122
training of journalists, 74
traits of journalists, 74–85
transposability, 11

Treaty of Versailles, 120
Trenchard, John, 30, 32
Truman, Harry S, 108, 124
turbonews, 8
Turning the Tide, 22
Twin Towers, 9, 56
two-valued logic, 33

undercover reporting, 75
UNESCO, 40–42
unrestricted submarine warfare, 119
USA Today, 50–51

Van kaveren, Adrian, 133
Veterans Affairs hospitals, 1
Viet Cong, 125
Vietnam, 9, 10, 124–128
Vietnam coverage, 126–127
Vietnam protest, 126
village reporting, 81–82
violence and public health, 60–62
Violence Assessment Monitoring
    Project, 57–58
virtual journalism, 82–83
visual determinism, 10
Vultee, Fred, 65–66

Wahhabism, 64
Wallace, Mike, 142–143
Walter Reed Army Medical Center, 1
Washington Post, 5
Washington press corps, 105
Watch Blog, 22
watchdog role of media, 75, 138

Watergate, 47, 50, 78, 139–141
Web and politics, 20–23
Web logs, 22
Webster, Noah, 98
Weiner, Robert, 129
West Wing, 99
Westmoreland, William, 125, 127
White House coverage, 105–107
Wigand, Jeffrey, 47–48, 141–143
Wikipedia, 21
William Allen White, 121
Williams, Jody, 2
Wilson, Woodrow, 7, 106, 107–108,
    118–120
Wolfe, Tom, 79–80
women journalists, 75
Wonkette, 22
Woodruff, Bob, 1, 79
Woodward, Bob, 5, 78, 139–141
World War I and the media, 118–120
World War II and the media,
    120–124
World War II coverage, 123

Xinhua News Agency, 38

Yago, Gideon, 19
Yankelovich, Daniel, 62
youth voting patterns, 59–62
YouTube, 21

Zepp's Last Stand, 49
Zimmerman note, 119

ABOUT THE AUTHOR

JIM WILLIS is a former newspaper reporter and editor for the *Oklahoman* and the *Dallas Morning News* who has been teaching journalism at the university level since 1978. He holds a Ph.D. in Journalism from the University of Missouri. He has held numerous faculty posts at Azusa Pacific University, Ashland University, and Northeastern Univiersity, and has held endowed chairs at the University of Oklahoma and the University of Memphis. He is a former Communication Department chair at Boston College and has been guest professor of American Media at Johannes Gutenberg University in Mainz, Germany, and Justus Liebig University in Giessen, Germany. Since leaving the practice of full-time daily journalism, he has covered numerous stories, including the bombing of the Alfred P. Murrah Federal Building in Oklahoma City. This is his ninth book on journalism and the news media.